S0-BIH-958

Whether you eat meat or dine strictly vegetarian, the recipes and information in this unusual book will save your food money while adding well-balanced nutrition and exciting flavors to your meals.

When Karen Brooks decided several years ago that meat eating was not for her, she also decided that the foods she would eat instead must be rich in nutrition and flavor. And how well she has succeeded!

This is vegetarian eating with a gourmet flair—mouth-watering specialties with marvelously clear instructions. And, as a bonus, the author includes a guide to the essential amino acids every adult needs, as well as a list of the protein content in more than one hundred non-meat foods.

The dishes she has created are made exclusively with natural ingredients—no white sugar, synthetic flavorings, or preservatives. So whether you want to plan an occasional meatless meal or intend to do without meat entirely, let Karen's recipes show you the way to the best food you ever ate!

THE COMPLETE VEGETARIAN COOKBOOK was originally published by Rodale Press, Inc.

The Complete Vegetarian Cookbook

(Original title: *The Forget-About-Meat Cookbook*)

Karen Brooks

PUBLISHED BY POCKET BOOKS NEW YORK

THE COMPLETE VEGETARIAN COOKBOOK

Rodale Press edition published 1974

POCKET BOOK edition published July, 1976

This POCKET BOOK edition includes every word contained in
the original, higher-priced edition. It is printed from brand-
new plates made from completely reset, clear, easy-to-read type.

POCKET BOOK editions are published by
POCKET BOOKS,
a division of Simon & Schuster, Inc.,
A GULF+WESTERN COMPANY
630 Fifth Avenue,
New York, N.Y. 10020.
Trademarks registered in the United States
and other countries.

Book design by Donald E. Breter.

Printed in the U.S.A.

Acknowledgments

To my dog Pringel who buried my first homemade bagel. And to my parents whose encouragement and aid brought this book to its completion.

I should like to express my thanks for the valuable contributions, suggestions, and assistance given to me by:

Lynn Clements
Judy Menthe
Lillian Zavadil
Edna Banker
Bill Tarr and those who cooked with me at Barnetts
The "guinea pigs" at Rainbow Ridge Farm . . . and
    Daniel

Contents

The
Complete Vegetarian
Cookbook

Introduction

When I was 18 years old, and going away to college, I decided to become a vegetarian. Unfortunately, I knew absolutely nothing about meat substitutes nor how to plan my diet. I had no idea how to get the protein that meat had supplied to my body. As a result I ate unbalanced meals that lacked many essential nutrients. During my first semester, I was always tired – a prime target for colds and other ailments. That was lesson enough for me. I have spent the past six years learning to supplement my diet in order to maintain good health and stamina and still refrain from eating meat. The recipes in this book reflect my efforts.

My first cooking instructions came from Lucy Phillips Blake whom I met when I was a student at the University of Missouri. I marvelled at the way she made her own bread and how she moved about the kitchen with such grace and confidence. We spent many hours together—cooking, experimenting with new recipes, and sharing our culinary secrets and techniques. I asked Lucy to contribute some of her recipes to this book so that you might enjoy them as I have.

When I left college, I moved to Easley, Missouri and lived at Rainbow Ridge, a 120-acre farm next to the Missouri River. We raised a tremendous variety of vegetables there. And although no pesticides were used, surprisingly little was lost to the bugs. As a matter of fact, there was such an abundance of everything that I began concocting new recipes daily just to make use of all the wonderful, fresh crops.

The peach and apple trees were heavy with fruit, and we already had so many blackberries that we were kept busy making fruit pies of every description. We made fruit butters and jams in addition to canning vegetables. By the time I left Easley, to become the manager of Barnett's Health Food Restaurant in Columbia, Missouri, I felt completely at home in the kitchen.

At Barnett's, I baked eight to ten loaves of bread a day plus pies, cakes and dinner specialties. I avoided using prepared or packaged products as much as possible, preferring instead to make my own foods such as granola cereal*, yogurt*, and mayonnaise*. Beans and seeds were sprouted to be used as garnishes for salads and sandwiches. My Strawberry-and-Banana Pie* was so well liked that, because of it, I was selected the "Cook-Of-The-Week" by the Columbia *Tribune*.

At the same time, my homemade breads, desserts, and granola cereal were rapidly gaining popularity. People gave me weekly orders for them. I was soon catering many of the local parties.

After I left Columbia and the restaurant business, I visited a wonderful family in East Troy, Wisconsin, by the name of Vanderploeg. Their beautiful farm had acres of apple trees, but the one that particularly caught my eye was a crab apple tree in the backyard. Although I had never used crab apples before, I proceeded to make four quarts of crab apple-apple butter*. It was delicious.

Mrs. Vanderploeg and I became close friends. I admired her style of cooking. She could make the most simple meal seem elegant. She graciously gave me several

2

of her favorite recipes, and you will find two of them—her Health Bread* and her Apple Bread*—in this book.

One of the secrets of good cooking is knowing how to flavor food. Amounts and types of spices are only guidelines in most recipes. Don't be afraid to adjust them or add a few seasonings according to your own taste. But remember flavoring should be a subtle thing. The trick is to maintain a balance so that no one flavor overpowers the others.

I have written this book to share some important ideas about foods and to prove that healthful, meatless dishes can be as appetizing and delicious as any of your family favorites.

Aspen, Colorado 1973

*See index for recipe

Chapter 1

Kitchen Clues

Carving Out Your Kitchen

To Equip Your Kitchen

1) two or three cast iron skillets (never put soap in these)
2) good mixing bowls—crocks or wooden ones
3) about four wooden spoons (one with a long handle)
4) measuring spoons
5) good, sharp knives (a long bladed one for slicing bread, vegetable knives, two pairing knives)
6) Pyrex measuring cups
7) portable cutting board (no cracks on the surface— keep it dry to prevent warping)
8) grater—a four sided one is best
9) potato masher
10) pastry blender
11) at least two bread pans
12) a large square baking pan
13) at least two round cake pans
14) soup pot (cast iron Dutch oven is best, but enamel will do in a pinch)
15) saucepans (three basic sizes with tight fitting lids)
16) one ladle
17) one slotted spoon

18) one large and one small strainer
19) jars for storing
20) blender
21) heavy ceramic teapot
22) spatula
23) pie plates
24) tongs
25) can opener
26) rolling pin
27) colander
28) muffin pan

Nice To Have—But Not Essential

29) double boiler
30) juicer
31) pressure cooker
32) eggbeater
33) wire whisk
34) vegetable scrub brush
35) cooling rack
36) mortar and pestle
37) waffle iron
38) tube pan
39) canisters
40) food grinder
41) corn stick cast iron pan
42) round pizza pan
43) yogurt maker—regulates temperature
44) Chinese *wok*—for cooking vegetables

Never use aluminum pots or pans; the metal can migrate into food during cooking. Glass or stainless steel are the best materials for cooking utensils.

Helpful Hints

1) Spaghetti, noodles and macaroni will not boil over or stick together as readily if one tablespoon of oil is put in the cooking water. This is a must for lasagna noodles or large noodles to be stuffed.

2) Green peppers will keep fresh longer if seeds are removed before storing peppers.

3) Vegetables stay fresh longer if they are not washed until just before they are used. Of course, the sooner they are used after picking, the better the flavor and the higher their nutritional content.

4) To blanch almonds cover them with boiling water, let stand a few minutes, drain and place almonds in a bowl of cold water. Rub the skins off with your fingers.

5) Olive oil is good for sautéing vegetables.

6) To make herb butter, use ½ cup herbs to 1 cup butter. Let butter soften, stir in herbs and chill.

7) To make onion juice, cut a slice from an onion and salt the cut end. Turn onion clockwise on a grater and juice will come out.

8) When you are using only half of an onion, save the root half—it will stay fresh longer.

9) When just a squeeze of lemon juice is needed, stick the lemon with a fork to get juice rather than slice the lemon. This will keep it fresh longer.

10) Place a raw potato or slice of bread in your refrigerator. It will absorb odors.

Equivalents

Butter   2 cups = 1 pound
                        8 tablespoons = ¼ pound

Coconut   5 cups (shredded) = 1 pound

Cheese   5 cups (freshly grated) = 1 pound

Cottage Cheese   2 cups = 1 pound

Dates   2½ cups (pitted) = 1 pound

Figs   2⅔ cups (chopped) = 1 pound

Flour, bread   3½-4 cups = 1 pound (except rye
                        which takes 6 cups to 1 pound)

1 Lemon, juiced   2-3 tablespoons juice
                        plus 2 teaspoons rind

Macaroni   1 cup uncooked = 2 to 2¼ cups
                        cooked
                        4 cups uncooked = 1 pound un-
                        cooked

Rice (Long
grained)   2½ cups uncooked = 1 pound

Dried Fruit   2 cups apricots = ½ pound
                        2 cups prunes (with pits) = 12
                        ounces
                        2 cups raisins = 10 ounces
                        2 cups dates (with pits) = 13
                        ounces

Carob	2⅔ cups carob = 1 pound

Eggs	3 medium = ½ cup

3 teaspoons	= 1 tablespoon
4 tablespoons	= ¼ cup
5⅓ tablespoons	= ⅓ cup
8 tablespoons	= ½ cup (4 fluid ounces)
16 tablespoons	= 1 cup (8 fluid ounces)
1 cup	= ½ pint
2 cups	= 1 pint
2 pints	= 1 quart
1 fluid ounce	= 2 tablespoons
16 ounces	= 1 pint (2 cups)
4 quarts	= 1 gallon (liquid)
8 quarts	= 1 peck (solid)
dash	= less than ⅛ teaspoon
4 cups dry milk	= 1 pound
1½ cups honey	= 1 pound
2 cups maple syrup	= 1 pound
1 cup molasses (blackstrap)	= 12 ounces
(cane molasses)	= 8 ounces
2 cups oil	= 1 pound
4 cups wheat germ	= 14 ounces

In reading these recipes, you may come across ingredients which are not familiar to you. All these ingredients should be available at health food stores and some at local grocery stores.

Arrowroot has practically no taste. It is an excellent thickening agent.

Baking Powder is substituted for baking soda in my recipes. Although even my homemade baking powder contains some bicarbonate of soda, it is a minimal amount.

Brewer's Yeast is a good source of protein and of the B-complex vitamins.

Carob Powder, also known as St. John's Bread, was a source of nutrition in biblical days. It is a substitute for chocolate or cocoa.

Kelp is derived from the sea. Besides being very rich minerally, it is a good source of iodine.

Pero is a coffee substitute made out of barley and rye grains.

Mu Tea has a gingery-licorice taste. This blend of many herbs is a delicious and unusual tea.

Safflower Shortening is made with 100% pure oil from the safflower plant. It is a good substitute for butter in cooking and baking.

Tamari Soy Sauce has no chemicals in it. It is made from water, soybeans, wheat and sea salt.

Tiger's Milk is made from a combination of natural protein sources such as milk, whey, and Brewer's yeast. It comes plain or carob flavored.

Unbleached White Flour is not as desirable, nutritionally, as whole wheat flour. However, I have found that adding it in combination with wheat flour for bread or desserts does produce a lighter texture. Add ¼ cup wheat germ to each ¾ cup of unbleached white flour to equal one cup of flour.

Wheat-Soy Macaroni is made with whole wheat and soy flours instead of white-enriched flour.

When To Use Herbs and Seasonings

ALLSPICE
  Desserts
  Preserves
  Catsup
  Spice Cakes
  Curry

ANISE SEED
  Cookies
  Coffee Cake
  Rye Bread
  Tea

BAY LEAVES
  Soups
  Potatoes
  Vegetable Stews
  Steamed Vegetables

BASIL
  Soups
  Vegetables
  Eggplant
  Peas
  Beans
  Tomato Dishes
  Sauces
  Salad Dressings
  Cheese Dishes
  Pizza
  Tea

CAYENNE PEPPER
  Use in place of black
  pepper, but in smaller
  amounts

CARAWAY SEED
Breads (rye)
Cottage Cheese
Salads
Coleslaw
Rice
Cabbage Dishes
Yogurt Dressing
Noodle Dishes
Tea

CARDAMOM SEED
Coffee Cake
Curry
Bread, Rolls
Apple Pie
Yogurt
Tea

CELERY SEED
Soups
Stuffing
Coleslaw
Potato Salad
Mayonnaise
Casseroles

CORIANDER
Cookies
Cakes
Candies
Salads
Curry
Tea

CINNAMON
Oatmeal
Desserts
Apple Dishes
Fruit Dishes
Rice Pudding
Breads
Tea

CLOVES
Cakes
Pumpkin Pie
Cider
Tea

CUMIN
Gravies
Soyburgers
Beans
Lentils
Mexican Dishes
Chili
Cabbage

CURRY POWDER
Rice
Contains:
    Allspice,
    Tumeric,
    Coriander,
    Dry Mustard,
    Cardamom

DILL WEED
- Cheese Dishes
- Oil-Vinegar Dressing
- Egg Dishes
- Salad
- Vegetable Stew

FENNEL
- Bread, Rolls
- Cakes
- Cookies
- Egg Dishes
- Soups
- Salad
- Beans
- Tea

GARLIC
- Italian Dishes
- Avocado
- Grainburgers
- Soyburgers
- Mashed Potatoes
- Beans
- Salad
- Dressing
- Vegetables
- Bread
- Soup
- Sauces

GINGER
- Bread
- Cake
- St. John Patties
- Pumpkin Pie
- Pickling
- Chinese Vegetables
- Grapefruit
- Fruit Dishes
- Pudding
- Tea

PAPRIKA
- Hash Browns
- Fried Potatoes
- Deviled Eggs
- Salads
- Vegetables
- Cottage Cheese
- Casseroles
- Stuffed Peppers
- Rice

MACE
- Spice Cakes
- Pumpkin Pie
- Cookies

SAGE
- Dressing
- Lentils
- Rice
- Cottage Cheese
- Tea

13

TARRAGON
Egg Dishes
Tomato Dishes
Green Salad
Vinegar

MINT
Yogurt
Cold Soup
Vegetables
Glazed Carrots
Ice Cream
Tea

SAVORY
Scrambled Eggs
Beans
Bean Salad
Lentils
String Beans

THYME
Onion Soup
Soup
Rice
Potatoes
Green Beans
Onions
Cheese Dishes
Carrots
Peas

MARJORAM
Vegetable Stew
Soups
Salad
Cottage Cheese
Spinach
Squash
Green Beans
Egg Dishes

OREGANO
Chili
Mexican Dishes
Beans
Gravy
Tomato Dishes
Pizza
Italian Foods
Vegetables

NUTMEG
Custard
Mushrooms
Eggnog
Cheese Dishes
Apple Pie
Desserts

PARSLEY
Potato Soup
Salads
Egg Dishes
Casseroles
Bread Stuffing

TURMERIC
- Cream Sauce
- With ginger in pickling

SESAME AND SUN-FLOWER SEEDS
- Desserts
- Breads
- Fruit Salads
- Cereals
- Pie Crusts
- Salads
- Casseroles

ROSEMARY
- Soups
- Fruit Salad Dressing
- Vinegars
- Vegetables
- Peas
- Stuffing
- Sauces

Note: Use the amount of seasonings suggested in recipes as a guideline. Flavoring is a matter of individual taste. Feel free to adjust seasonings to your taste.

Sprouted Seeds and Beans

Method 1 Cheesecloth

1. Wash and soak seeds or beans in water 4 to 6 hours. Drain water.
2. Spread a clean, damp cheesecloth on a flat surface, such as a tray.
3. Spread beans or seeds over damp cloth and cover with another damp cheesecloth.
4. Always keep the cloth damp by pouring cool water over it when needed and tipping the tray into the sink to drain. Do this at least 4 times daily.
5. Lift the cloth after 3 or 4 days; seeds or beans should be sprouted.
6. Sprouts should be at least the length of the seed.

Method 2 Jar

1. Put beans or seeds in a sterilized jar.
2. Soak the beans/seeds 4 to 6 hours.
3. Cover top with a cheesecloth or stocking secured with an elastic band, or the jar's lid with holes punched in it.
4. Drain water through lid or cloth.
5. Soak the beans about 5 minutes, at least three times a day to prevent them from drying out, and drain water as above. Use cool water for soaking.
   Note: Seeds or beans may be soaked more than 3 times a day if they seem to be drying out.
6. Repeat for several days till sprouts are at least the length of the seed or bean.
   Note: Sprout at room temperature.

Notes on Sprouts:

1. Try sprouting wheat and rye berries, sunflower, sesame and alfalfa seeds, mung beans, soybeans, lentils or garbanzo beans.
2. Use sprouts in soups, salads, sandwiches, omelets, *chop suey*, breads, pancakes, etc.
3. Sprouts are very economical.
4. Sprouts are a rich source of vitamin C.
5. Sprouts are not only high in vitamins, they are rich in minerals.

Notes on Milk:

1. Certified raw milk is one of the best milks to use. It may be bought at health foods stores and some grocery stores.
2. Non-fat dry milk is better for you than whole milk, so is skimmed or low-fat milk.
3. To sour milk: Add 1 to 2 tablespoons lemon juice or vinegar to 1 cup of milk. Let it stand for a few minutes.

Grain Texture Chart

Grain	Texture	Uses for Cooking	Distinctions—Hints
Whole wheat	semi-heavy	breads, pancakes, desserts, any recipe calling for flour	Gluten content is high. Contains: wheat germ, B & E vitamins, calcium, phosphorus, and protein. Use ⅛ cup less when substituting for white flour.
Rye	fine grain, heavy	pancakes, breads, pumpernickel, muffins, biscuits. Combines well with other grains. Try in banana bread (small amount)	Gluten content is fair. Contains: sodium, phosphorus, chlorine. Combines well with buckwheat or wholewheat.
Unbleached white	light, very fine	Mix with other grains for lighter texture. Pastry baking and with heavy flours, makes pie crust easier to roll out.	Wheat germ and bran has been removed so supplement these to make up the loss. Add ⅓ cup wheat germ or ¼ cup bran to 1 cup flour. Then directed amount of liquid should be increased by ¼ cup.
Oats	moist, chewy, heavy, creamy	breads, granola, dessert topping, binding for rice and soyburgers, cereal muffins. Combine with other grains for baking.	Good source of protein.

Grain Texture Chart—Continued

Grain	Texture	Uses for Cooking	Distinctions—Hints
Buckwheat	very heavy, fine grain	bread—usually not more than a cup. pancakes. Soup or sauce thickener.	Rich in protein, good with sourdough, contains silicon.
Soy Brown rice Barley Potato	moist, heavy	Small amounts in bread, no more than 1 cup usually. Thickening for soups and sauces.	Contains protein and calcium—a good source of vitamins, minerals and amino acids.
Cornmeal	semi-heavy crunchy, can be gritty, depending on grind.	Cornbread, breads combined with other grains, pancakes, good in chapatti combined with wheat flour.	Yellow is more nutritious than white. Indian meal is cornmeal with chia seeds and sunflower seeds.

Protein Planning

If you really plan to forget about eating meat on a regular basis, it is necessary to evaluate the quality of protein in the food you eat. Protein quality depends on how much of each of the basic elements (amino acids) of protein a food contains. Of the twenty-two amino acids, eight (tryptophan, leucine, isoleucine, lysine, valine, threonine, phenylalanine, methionine) have been designated as absolutely essential for adult humans to get through diet. The remaining fourteen amino acids are synthesized in your body as needed. Together they make up the protein combinations that become skin, eyes, hair, vital organs, etc.

All of the so-called essential amino acids occur in perfect combination in any single meat or fish food. Vegetable foods and dairy products also contain amino acids in varying combinations and values, but no one of them contains all the essential amino acids in meaningful amounts.

Of course, the answer is to choose foods that offer complementary amino acids. But this takes planning. The amount of complete protein absorbed by the body is dictated by the lowest common denominator of the essential amino acids. For example, a meal that consists of yams, cabbage and eggplant yields only about 100 milligrams of valine, an essential amino acid. In this case valine is the lowest common denominator and regardless of the other amino acid values in these foods, the total amount of protein absorbed by the body is dictated by that 100 milligrams of valine. To use the other amino acids in the meal efficiently, you would have to increase the amount of valine, by adding some valine-rich food, such as egg, peas or nuts.

Another caution: You can't fill in the amino acids missing at lunch by eating them at dinner. All essential amino acids must be consumed at the same time.

The following charts show the recommended daily intake of each essential amino acid and the amount of each contained in the foods listed. This information will help you to plan meatless meals that have a full complement of protein.

Essential Amino Acids
Daily Intake

Source: Heinz Handbook of Nutrition

Essential Amino Acids	Recommended Daily Intake Milligrams	Minimum Daily Intake Men Milligrams	Minimum Daily Intake Women Milligrams
Phenylalanine	2,200	1,100	220
Methionine	2,200	1,100	290
Leucine	2,200	1,100	620
Valine	1,600	800	650
Lysine	1,600	800	500
Isoleucine	1,400	700	450
Threonine	1,000	500	310
Tryptophan	500	250	160

Essential Amino Acid Content of Foods

Sources: Heinz Handbook of Nutrition and Amino Acid Content of Foods, a U.S.D.A. Publication, Research Report #4.
*Histidine may be an essential amino acid for children but not for adults.
Amino Acid content of foods is expressed in milligrams per 100 grams (3½ ozs.) edible portion.

Food	Histidine*	Threonine	Valine	Leucine	Isoleucine	Lysine	Methionine	Phenylaline	Tryptophan
EGGS, whole (chicken)	307	637	950	1,126	850	819	401	739	211
FRUITS									
avocados	—	—	—	—	—	74	12	—	14
bananas	—	—	—	—	—	55	11	—	18
dates	49	61	94	77	74	65	27	63	61
grapefruit	—	—	—	—	—	6	—	—	1
limes	—	—	—	—	—	15	2	—	3
oranges	—	—	—	—	—	24	3	—	3
papayas	—	—	—	—	—	38	2	—	12
pineapples	—	—	—	—	—	9	1	—	5
GRAINS									
barley	239	433	643	889	545	433	184	661	160
buckwheat flour (dark)	256	461	607	683	440	687	206	442	165

Essential Amino Acid Content of Foods—Continued

Food	Histidine*	Threonine	Valine	Leucine	Isoleucine	Lysine	Methionine	Phenylalanine	Tryptophan
corn, field	206	398	510	1,296	462	288	186	454	61
corn flour	161	311	398	1,011	361	225	145	354	47
corn grits	180	347	444	1,128	402	251	161	395	53
corn flakes	226	275	386	1,047	306	154	135	354	52
corn germ	464	622	789	1,030	578	791	232	483	144
corn gluten	200	344	512	1,563	443	179	282	558	59
corn hominy	203	316	398	810	349	358	99	333	84
cornmeal (whole ground)	190	367	470	1,192	425	265	171	418	56
corn tortilla	128	235	304	939	345	145	111	252	31
millet (foxtail)	218	323	717	1,737	790	218	291	697	103
millet (pearl millet)	240	456	682	1,746	635	383	270	506	248
oatmeal and rolled oats	261	470	845	1,065	733	521	209	758	183
rice, brown	126	294	524	646	352	296	135	377	81
rice, white and converted	128	298	531	655	356	300	137	382	82
rice flakes or puffed	137	—	—	—	—	56	—	286	46

rice germ	430	2,177	938	838	630	1,707	420	750	270
rye	276	448	631	813	515	494	191	571	137
rye flour, light	214	348	490	632	400	348	148	443	106
rye flour, dark	260	422	594	766	485	465	180	538	129
sorghum	211	394	628	1,767	598	299	190	547	123
wheat, durum	259	366	588	852	551	348	194	627	157
wheat, hard red spring	286	403	648	939	607	384	214	691	173
wheat, hard red winter	251	354	570	825	534	338	188	608	152
wheat, soft red winter	208	294	472	684	443	280	156	504	126
white	192	271	435	630	408	258	143	464	116
wheat flour (whole-grain)	271	383	616	892	577	365	203	657	164
LEGUMES									
chickpeas	559	739	1,025	1,538	1,195	1,434	276	1,012	170
cowpeas	692	901	1,293	1,715	1,110	1,491	352	1,198	220
kidney beans, red raw	658	1,002	1,401	1,985	1,312	1,715	233	1,275	214
lentils	548	896	1,360	1,760	1,316	1,528	180	1,104	216

Amino Acid content of foods is expressed in milligrams per 100 grams (3½ ozs.) edible portion.

Essential Amino Acid Content of Foods—Continued

Food	Histidine*	Threonine	Valine	Leucine	Isoleucine	Lysine	Methionine	Phenylaldine	Tryptophan
lima beans	669	980	1,298	1,722	1,199	1,378	331	1,222	195
mung beans	543	765	1,444	2,202	1,351	1,667	265	1,167	180
peanuts	749	828	1,532	1,872	1,266	1,099	271	1,557	340
peanut butter	727	803	1,487	1,816	1,228	1,066	263	1,510	330
peanut flour	1,425	1,575	2,916	3,563	2,410	2,091	516	2,963	647
peas	651	918	1,333	1,969	1,340	1,744	286	1,200	251
soybeans	911	1,504	2,005	2,946	2,054	2,414	513	1,889	526
soybean curd	—	—	—	—	—	—	81	—	—
soybean flour	1,166	1,926	2,568	3,773	2,630	3,092	658	2,419	673
soybean milk	121	176	186	305	175	269	54	195	51
soybean sprouts	133	159	225	265	225	211	45	186	—
MILK									
buttermilk	99	165	262	348	219	291	82	186	38
canned	185	323	481	688	447	545	171	340	99
casein	3,021	4,277	7,393	10,048	6,550	8,013	3,084	5,389	1,335
cow	92	161	240	344	223	272	86	170	49
dried, whole	680	1,191	1,774	2,535	1,648	2,009	632	1,251	364

goat	68	217	139	278	87	312	65	121	39
human	30	62	86	124	75	90	28	60	23

CHEESES

blue mold	701	799	1,543	2,096	1,449	1,577	559	1,153	293
camembert	571	650	1,256	1,706	1,179	1,284	455	938	239
cheddar	815	929	1,794	2,437	1,685	1,834	650	1,340	341
cheddar processed	756	862	1,665	2,262	1,563	1,702	604	1,244	316
cottage	549	794	978	1,826	989	1,428	469	917	179
cream cheese	278	408	538	923	519	721	229	547	80
limburger	691	788	1,522	2,067	1,429	1,555	552	1,136	289
Parmesan	1,174	1,337	2,584	3,510	2,426	2,641	937	1,930	491
Swiss	896	1,021	1,974	2,681	1,853	2,017	715	1,474	375
Swiss processed	861	981	1,895	2,574	1,779	1,937	687	1,415	360
whey, dried	159	677	640	1,043	734	769	188	323	147

NUTS

acorns	251	434	718	808	561	636	139	473	126
almonds	517	610	1,124	1,454	873	582	259	1,146	176
Brazil nuts	367	422	823	1,129	593	443	941	617	187
cashews	415	737	1,592	1,522	1,222	792	353	946	471

Amino Acid content of foods is expressed in milligrams per 100 grams (3½ ozs.) edible portion.

Essential Amino Acid Content of Foods—Continued

Food	Histidine*	Threonine	Valine	Leucine	Isoleucine	Lysine	Methionine	Phenylaline	Tryptophan
coconut	69	129	212	269	180	152	71	174	33
cottonseed flour and meal	1,325	1,764	2,458	2,945	1,884	2,139	686	2,610	591
filberts	288	415	934	939	853	417	139	537	211
pecans	273	389	525	773	553	435	153	564	138
pumpkin seeds	711	933	1,679	2,437	1,737	1,411	577	1,749	560
safflower seed meal	985	1,462	2,446	2,740	1,914	1,525	731	2,605	675
sesame seeds	441	707	885	1,679	951	583	637	1,457	331
sesame seed meal	763	1,223	1,531	2,905	1,645	1,008	1,103	2,521	573
sunflower seeds	586	911	1,354	1,736	1,276	868	443	1,220	343
sunflower seed meal	1,006	1,565	2,325	2,981	2,191	1,491	760	2,094	589
walnuts (English or Persian)	405	589	974	1,228	767	441	306	767	175
LEAFY VEGETABLES (RAW)									
beet greens	26	76	101	129	84	108	34	116	24
brussels sprouts	106	153	193	194	186	197	46	148	44

cabbage	25	39	43	57	40	66	13	30	11
chard	18	58	55	76	60	55	4	46	14
collards	87	114	195	218	121	202	46	124	55
kale	62	139	184	252	133	121	35	158	42
lettuce						70	4		12
mustard greens	41	60	108	62	75	111	24	75	37
parsley						160	12		50
spinach	49	102	126	176	107	142	39	99	37
watercress	34	84	84	131	76	91	10	62	28
OTHER RAW VEGETABLES									
asparagus	36	66	106	96	80	103	32	69	27
beans, snap	45	91	115	139	109	126	35	57	33
beets	22	34	49	55	51	86	6	27	14
broccoli	63	122	170	163	126	147	50	119	37
carrots	17	43	56	65	46	52	10	42	10
cauliflower	48	102	144	162	104	134	47	75	33
celery						21	15		12
cucumbers	1	19	24	30	22	31	7	16	5
eggplant	19	38	65	68	56	30	6	48	10

Amino Acid content of foods is expressed in milligrams per 100 grams (3½ ozs.) edible portion.

Essential Amino Acid Content of Foods—Continued

Food	Histi-dine*	Threo-nine	Valine	Leucine	Iso-leucine	Lysine	Methio-nine	Phenyl-alanine	Trypto-phan
mushrooms (Agaricus campestris)	—	—	378	281	532	—	167	—	6
okra	30	66	91	101	69	76	22	65	18
onions	14	22	31	37	21	64	13	39	21
peppers	14	50	33	46	46	51	16	55	9
pumpkin	19	28	45	63	44	58	11	32	16
radishes	—	59	30	—	—	34	2	—	5
squash	9	14	22	27	19	23	8	16	5
tomatoes	15	33	28	41	29	42	7	28	9
turnips	—	—	—	—	20	57	12	20	—
STARCHY ROOTS AND TUBERS									
potatoes, raw	29	79	107	100	88	107	25	88	21
potato flour	102	279	379	353	311	378	89	314	76
sweet potatoes, raw	36	85	135	103	87	85	33	100	31
yams	—	—	—	—	—	110	34	—	35

Chapter 2

Do-It-Yourselves

This collection of recipes is presented first because many of them are used in making other recipes throughout the book.

Apple Sauce (cooked)

2 medium-sized apples, peeled, cored and finely-chopped
¼ cup water
  cinnamon to taste
½ teaspoon honey
  squeeze of fresh lemon juice

Peel and slice apples, removing seeds and core. Place apples in a saucepan and add enough water to prevent burning and sticking (approximately ¼ amount of apples). Cook over low flame 8 to 10 minutes until soft. Press through a sieve or whirl in a blender. Add cinnamon, honey and lemon juice. Serve with raisins.

Yield: 1 cup

Apple Sauce (uncooked blender-style)

> 2 medium-sized red apples, peeled, cored and finely-chopped
> 1 teaspoon honey
> ¼ cup apple juice
> ½ teaspoon cinnamon
> ½ teaspoon nutmeg
> squeeze of lime juice

> Blend all ingredients in blender till smooth. Try *Apple Sauce Spice Cake* with this apple sauce and you'll be delighted with the results.

> Yield: 1 cup

Pear Sauce

> Follow either of the preceding rules for apple sauce, but replace apples with pears and add a dash of cloves.

Crab Apple-Apple Butter

> 6 cups crab apples with skins
> 6 cups red apples with skins
> 2 tablespoons apple cider vinegar
> honey to taste (at least 1 pound)
> 1 tablespoon cinnamon

> Cut apples into small chunks, removing seeds and core. Place apples in a soup pot with enough water to cover apples. Begin cooking over a low flame. Mix in vinegar. Stir occasionally to prevent sticking. When chunks

are cooked down smooth begin adding honey, little by little, till desired sweetness is reached. Keep cooking, stirring occasionally, till browned (will take 3 to 4 hours). Add cinnamon. Press through a sieve or partially blend in blender for chunky texture. When cooled, store apple butter in sterilized, air-tight jars.

Yield: approximately 2 quarts

Peach Butter

10 cups ripe peaches
2½-2¾ cups water
2 teaspoons cinnamon
1 teaspoon nutmeg
1 teaspoon cloves
honey to taste (about 4 cups)

Wash peaches. Remove pits and cut peaches into small pieces leaving the skins on. Put peaches in soup pot and cover with water. Cook over low flame till smooth and turning brown, about 4 to 5 hours, stirring occasionally to prevent sticking. Add spices and honey slowly to reach desired sweetness. When cooled, pour peach butter into sterilized, airtight jars. This is delicious and easy to make but requires attention, so be prepared to spend the day at home!

Yield: approximately 1½-2 quarts

Dried Apples

Slice whole apples in thin slices (circles). Cut out a small hole in the center of each circle, run a string through all the holes and hang the apple rings up to dry indoors (7 to 14 days). An alternative method is placing the apple rings on a tray outside in semishade for 5 to 7 days, bringing the tray indoors each night and on rainy days.

Note: The moisture is out of the apples in 24 hours but it actually takes this many days for the drying process to be completed.

Barbecue Sauce

¾ onion, chopped
¾ green pepper, chopped
½ cup celery, diced
1½ cups tomato juice
½ cup catsup
1 teaspoon Tamari soy sauce
1 teaspoon salt
  few dashes Tabasco sauce
⅛ teaspoon cayenne pepper
⅛ teaspoon paprika

Combine all the ingredients in a saucepan. Bring to a boil. Reduce heat and simmer 45 minutes or until thick. Pour sauce into a sterilized, quart jar and seal tightly with the lid.

Yield: approximately 1 quart

Old-Fashioned Peanut Butter

2½ cups raw peanuts
¼ cup oil
dash salt
½ teaspoon honey

Spread peanuts out on a lightly-oiled, shallow pan. Roast at 400° for 5 minutes. Remove from oven and while still warm put into blender, a few nuts at a time, with oil, salt, and about ½ teaspoon of honey. Blend till smooth, or leave partly crunchy. Store, covered, in refrigerator.

Yield: 1¾ cups

Basic Cream Sauce

2 tablespoons butter
2 tablespoons flour (wheat, soy, potato, etc.)
1 cup milk
½ teaspoon salt
dash cayenne pepper

In a saucepan, melt butter at low temperature. Remove pan from heat and stir in flour. Blend to make a paste. Return to heat and slowly add milk. Stir till thick and add salt and pepper.

Variations: 1. Add egg yolk for richer sauce. 2. Decrease to 1 tablespoon of flour and 1 tablespoon of butter for thinner sauce. 3. Add 1 tablespoon chopped onion to butter and lightly brown before adding flour. 4. Try garlic, parsley, nutmeg, a bay leaf or cloves for added flavor.

Yield: approximately 1 cup

Tomato Sauce

3 tablespoons chopped onion
1 clove garlic, chopped
2 tablespoons butter
3 tablespoons celery
3 cups stewed tomatoes
  salt to taste
  dash cayenne pepper
½ teaspoon thyme
½ teaspoon basil
½ teaspoon oregano
1 bay leaf

In a saucepan, brown the onions and garlic, lightly, in butter. Add the celery and sauté until tender. Add the tomatoes and the seasonings. Bring to a boil. Cover, reduce heat, and simmer slowly for an hour. Remove bay leaf.

Yield: 3 cups

Gravy

2½ tablespoons butter
1 tablespoon chopped onion
3 tablespoons flour (whole wheat, soy, potato, etc.)
¼ teaspoon honey
2½ cups stock
  salt and cayenne pepper to taste
1 teaspoon Tamari soy sauce (optional)

Mix all ingredients in a saucepan and simmer for 10 minutes.

Yield: 2½ cups

Blender Mayonnaise

2 eggs
1 teaspoon salt
1 tablespoon honey
6 tablespoons apple cider vinegar
2 cups oil

Blend all ingredients except oil on low speed until smooth. Add oil very slowly—this is important to keep oil from separating. Blend on low speed until well mixed.

Yield: 2½ cups

Lemon Curd

1 lemon rind, grated
2 eggs, beaten
¼ cup butter
1 cup honey
juice of two lemons

In the top of a double boiler, over boiling water, put lemon rind, beaten eggs, butter, honey, and lemon juice. Stir constantly until mixture thickens. Be careful not to burn. Cool and spread on toast or serve warm on cake. For a special treat try lemon curd spread over gingerbread.

Yield: 1½ cups

Basic Cheese Sauce

Follow directions for *Basic Cream Sauce* and add 1 cup of grated, unprocessed cheese after milk has thickened. Stir till all the cheese has melted.

Yield: approximately 2 cups

Vermont-Style Mustard

1¼ pounds dry mustard
⅛ pound soy flour
⅛ pound whole wheat flour
4 level teaspoons salt
7 teaspoons honey
1 teaspoon turmeric
apple cider vinegar

Mix dry ingredients. Slowly add enough apple cider vinegar to make a paste. Put mustard in a pint jar and let it stand for 1 month before using.

Yield: approximately 1 pint

Chop Suey Pickles

6 large cucumbers, peeled and sliced
10 medium-sized onions, sliced in rings
3 large green peppers, sliced and seeds removed
3 large, sweet red peppers, sliced and seeds removed
½ cup salt
1 pint apple cider vinegar
3 tablespoons pickling spices
½ cup honey
1 tablespoon celery seed
1 teaspoon curry powder

Prepare cucumbers, onions, green and red peppers. Set aside. In a large pot, combine the remaining ingredients. Bring to a boil. Add vegetables and cook until tender. Sterilize 4 quart jars. With a sterilized wooden spoon, equally distribute the vegetables among the 4 jars. Fill with the liquid from the pot to within ½ inch from the top of each jar. Put sterilized caps on jars, securing tightly. Let stand 6 weeks before using.

Yield: 4 quarts

Purple Plum Butter

8 cups small purple plums, pitted and sliced into small pieces
1½ cups water
½ cup honey
1 teaspoon cinnamon

Simmer plums and water in a pot, stirring occasionally until thick—about 5 hours. Add honey and cinnamon. Cool to a warm temperature and put mixture in blender at low speed for a few minutes for a finer texture. Pour into a sterilized quart jar and seal tightly with cap.

Yield: 1 quart

Sour Cream Substitute

Add a few tablespoons of vinegar to a cup of powdered milk with a little extra powder added. Let stand for a few minutes in a warm place.

Yield: approximately 1 cup

Bread Stuffing

- 1 cup chopped onion
- 1 cup chopped celery
- ½ pound butter
- 1 pound loaf whole wheat bread (homemade is best), dried till it is hard—may be sliced and dried—in oven at low temperature till crisp
- 1-2 cups boiling water
- 2 eggs, beaten
- 1 teaspoon sage
  dash thyme
  dash marjoram
  salt and cayenne pepper to taste
- ¼ cup parsley
- 1 cup walnuts or pecans, chopped

Sauté onion and celery in butter. Add bread broken into small pieces. Add boiling water, eggs, seasoning, parsley, and nuts. Bake 1 hour or until brown and crusty on top, in 350° oven.

Variation: Add 1 cup sauteed mushrooms.

Yield: 6-8 servings

Rich Carob Yogurt

- 2 cups yogurt
- 2 tablespoons carob powder
- ¼ cup honey
- ½ teaspoon vanilla

Blend all ingredients till smooth.

Yield: 4 servings

Yogurt is a bacterial culture that aids digestion and has all the food value of milk. Be careful in your preparation of yogurt, as the culture is sensitive to heat and cold.

1. Measure the amount of milk you wish to turn into yogurt, plus 1½ tablespoons extra as this much usually evaporates.
2. Raw, skim, or nonfat powdered dry milk may be used.
3. Place the milk in the top of a double boiler.
4. Heat slowly to right under the boiling point —which is when tiny bubbles appear around the edges of the pan.
5. Remove from the heat immediately at this point.
6. Let milk cool to lukewarm—about 110°.
7. Stir in 2 tablespoons of culture for each quart of milk.

   Note: a) Culture is plain, fresh yogurt. Use a clean spoon to spoon it out.
   b) Do not add too much culture, as it will crowd the bacteria and interfere with its action.

8. Put yogurt in clean jars.
9. Set jars in a pan of lukewarm water and cover with a towel.
10. Keep in a warm place for 8 hours.
11. When yogurt thickens, refrigerate it.
12. This should keep 5 to 8 days before the culture deactivates itself.

Curry Dip

    1 cup *Blender Mayonnaise* (see index)
    1 teaspoon tarragon vinegar
    ½ teaspoon freshly-grated horseradish
    1 teaspoon grated onion
    ½ teaspoon Tamari soy sauce
    ¼ teaspoon garlic powder
    1 tablespoon curry powder

Mix all ingredients. Chill. Serve with raw vegetables such as cauliflowerets, celery sticks, carrot sticks.

Yield: 1 cup of dip

Guacamole Delight

    1 large, fresh tomato, skinned and finely-chopped
    4 green onions, finely-chopped
    juice of ½ lemon
    1 teaspoon Tamari soy sauce
    3 dashes Tabasco sauce
    ¾ teaspoon salt
    ¼ teaspoon pepper
    dash of cayenne pepper (optional)
    3 ripe avocados, skinned, pitted and mashed (save the pits)

Mix the tomato and onion together in a bowl. Add the next 6 ingredients. Mix together. Add avocado and mix well. To prevent discoloration, add the avocado pits. Cover and chill in refrigerator. Remove the pits just prior to serving. Place bowl on a plate and surround the bowl with corn chips.

Yield: 6 servings

Baking Powder

⅓ cup potassium bicarbonate
⅔ cup cream of tartar
⅔ cup arrowroot

Mix, sift and store in a jar.

Yield: about 2 cups

Note: If you do not make your own baking powder then I recommend Cellu baking powder as it has a low sodium content. Most other brands not only have a high sodium content, but also contain aluminum compounds which can be irritating to the stomach.

Chapter 3

Day Breakers

Granolas and Cereals

Granola is a wonderful way to start the day. This mixture of grains provides protein, B vitamins, vitamin E and calcium. It is body building, energy producing and has a delightful crunch.

Serve granola for breakfast with fresh fruit, milk or yogurt. Or use it anytime as a topping for ice cream, doughnuts, or cakes. If you're a peanut butter lover, add a teaspoon of peanut butter to a bowl of granola and top it off with banana slices. On a nippy morning you can enjoy hot cereal simply by adding boiling water to granola. Whatever way you care to serve it, granola's a tasty way to get nutrients.

When you make cereal be sure to mix it thoroughly.

Stored in tightly-closed glass jars, in a refrigerator, granola will keep for a long time.

Good Morning Breakfast—for one person

½ cup cooked oatmeal
2 tablespoons yogurt
1 teaspoon honey

Combine all ingredients. Top with chopped almonds, chopped apple or sesame seeds and raisins for added flavor and nutrition.

45

Granola Deluxe Style
Preheat oven: 300°

2 cups shredded coconut
7 cups rolled oats
1 cup sesame seeds
1 cup wheat germ
1 cup sunflower seeds
1 cup cashews
1 teaspoon cinnamon
¼ cup carob powder
1 cup sliced dates or figs
4 cups honey
1 tablespoon vanilla
1 cup pure oil
1 cup raisins

Mix the dry ingredients and dried fruit, except the raisins. Mix honey, vanilla and oil, and pour over dry mixture. Spread in oiled, shallow pans. Bake in preheated oven for 20 minutes or until evenly browned. Stir about every 10 minutes. If this recipe makes too much granola for your needs, just cut the ingredients in half.

Hint: To insure even toasting, don't spread in pans more than ½ inch high. Be careful not to overbake.
Add raisins after toasting is finished.

Yield: about 20 cups

Poor Man's Granola

6 cups rolled oats
2 cups bran flakes
3 cups wheat germ
3 cups sunflower seeds
¼ cup carob powder
1 cup oil
4 cups honey

Follow directions for *Granola Deluxe Style*.

Yield: about 19 cups

Uncooked Protein Cereal

2 cups oats
1 cup wheat germ
1 cup shredded coconut
½ cup almonds
½ cup pecans
1 tablespoon brewer's yeast
½ teaspoon kelp
2 tablespoons carob powder
½ cup honey
½ cup oil
1 tablespoon molasses

Mix ingredients and refrigerate.

Yield: 6 cups

Rice Cereal

For a hearty breakfast, mix leftover rice with honey and yogurt or milk (or just honey alone). Serve hot or cold.

47

Familia
Preheat oven: 350°

    1 cup crushed oats
    1 cup cracked wheat
    1 cup sesame seeds
    1 cup sunflower seeds
    1 cup raisins
    1 cup dried apples, cut in quarters
    3 tablespoons carob powder
    1 cup wheat germ

Mix ingredients and toast in shallow pans for about 10 minutes. Serve with honey and milk or yogurt.

Yield: 7 cups

Egg Dishes—General Information

BOILED EGGS:

Hard boiled: 15-20 minutes
Medium boiled: 5-10 minutes
Soft boiled: 3- 5 minutes

This timing is approximate depending on the size of the egg. This is for a medium-sized egg. Cover eggs with cold water and bring to a boil. Add a little salt to prevent the shells from cracking.

If an egg is fresh, it sinks to the bottom and lays on its side when placed in water.

DEVILED EGGS:

Hard boil eggs. Cool and slice in half. Remove yolk and mash with some mayonnaise and a little prepared mustard. Refill egg white centers with yolk mixture and top with paprika.

POACHED EGGS:

Fill a pot with lightly-salted water. Bring to a boil, then reduce heat to right under boiling point (not bubbling hard but just around the edges). Break an egg into a saucer and slowly slide the egg into the water. When the white is firm, carefully remove egg with slotted spoon. Serve on toast or on pancakes.

SCRAMBLED EGGS:

Beat eggs with milk or yogurt. If adding mushrooms, onions, or green pepper, lightly sauté the vegetables first. Pour mixture into skillet, stirring constantly with a wooden spoon. Eggs should be light and fluffy.

I strongly recommend the use of fresh, fertile farm eggs. Some grocery and health food stores carry them or will order them for you.

You can tell the difference in the quality of eggs by looking at the color of the yolk. Fresh eggs, from farms where the chickens are free to walk around, have a dark yellow yolk, whereas yolks from chickens who are permanently caged have a pale yellow hue.

Breakfast Egg Casserole
Preheat oven: 350°

> 4 hard boiled eggs, sliced
> ¼ pound raw mushrooms, sliced
> 2 tablespoons onion, chopped
> 1 tomato, thinly-sliced
> fresh sprigs parsley
> 1 teaspoon salt
> ½ teaspoon tarragon
> 1 cup *Basic Cheese Sauce* (see index)
> paprika
>
> Arrange all ingredients, except the cheese sauce and paprika, in a lightly-oiled casserole dish. Pour cheese sauce over all and top with paprika. Bake in preheated oven 12 minutes or until browned.
>
> Yield: 4 servings

Sprout Omelet

> 1 tablespoon peanut oil
> 1 tablespoon white cooking sherry
> dash ginger
> ¼ cup green onion, chopped
> ¼ cup green pepper, sliced
> ½ cup watercress (optional)
> 4 medium-sized eggs
> 1 cup sprouts (soybean or mung bean are especially good here)
>
> In a large skillet, with a cover, heat oil, sherry and ginger. Add onion and green pepper. Sauté about 2 minutes. Add watercress, 1 tablespoon of water and steam, covered, for

about ½ minute. In a mixing bowl, beat eggs, place the sprouts in them. Add to vegetable mixture. Cook, covered, over low heat. After a few minutes put some slits in the middle of the omelet to let the uncooked egg run to the bottom of the skillet. The omelet should take 10 minutes to cook. Slip under broiler a minute to set the remaining egg on top. Fold omelet and serve.

Yield: 4 servings

Lucy's Vegetable Omelet

2 tablespoons butter
1 cup mushrooms, chopped
1 green pepper, chopped
3 green onions, chopped
1 tomato, chopped
6 eggs
1-2 cups unprocessed cheese, grated

Sauté vegetables in butter, in a cast iron skillet, adding tomatoes last. In a medium-sized mixing bowl, beat eggs till they are lemon colored. Pour eggs into another oiled, prewarmed skillet and cook slowly lifting edges to allow uncooked part to run underneath. When all but top ¼ inch of eggs is set, add vegetables, then cheese. Put pan under broiler for a minute or so to melt the cheese and set top of eggs. Fold in half and serve immediately.

Yield: 3 servings

Scrambled Eggs and Mushrooms

2 tablespoons butter
¼ cup onion, finely-chopped
1 cup mushrooms, sliced
8 eggs
2 tablespoons butter
salt and pepper to taste

Melt 2 tablespoons of butter in a large skillet. Sauté onions and mushrooms until lightly-browned. In a mixing bowl, beat eggs until light and fluffy. Melt remaining 2 tablespoons of butter in the skillet. Add eggs and scramble. Add more butter if eggs begin to stick to pan. Add seasonings.

Yield: 4 servings

French Toast
(excellent made with homemade bread)

milk
2-3 eggs, beaten
6 slices wheat bread
cinnamon, to sprinkle on toast

Add a little milk to the beaten eggs. Dip both sides of bread in batter and place in oiled, preheated skillet, over medium heat. Cook until browned on both sides. Serve sprinkled with cinnamon.

Variation: Replace milk with orange juice or coconut milk and add grated coconut to batter. Serve with grated apple on top.

Yield: 6 slices

Creamed Eggs on Toast

2 eggs, hard-boiled
2 slices whole wheat bread (toasted)
1 cup *Basic Cream Sauce* (see index)
½ cup grated, cheddar cheese
   dash cayenne
   dash nutmeg

Cut the eggs into slices. Arrange the slices on top of toasted bread. Make basic cream sauce and add the grated cheese, cayenne and nutmeg. Pour sauce over the eggs. Place under broiler for 3 minutes or until sauce is lightly-browned.

Yield: 2 servings

Spanish Omelet

1½ tablespoons butter
4 eggs
   salt and pepper to taste
3 tablespoons *Barbecue Sauce* (see index)

Preheat a cast iron skillet and melt butter. Beat eggs with salt and pepper until they are lemon colored and frothy. Pour eggs into skillet and cook over low heat. With a spatula, lift the edges of the omelet after it has cooked several minutes to allow uncooked egg to run to the bottom of the skillet. Add barbecue sauce and spread it evenly over the top of the omelet. Slip omelet under broiler to heat sauce and cook any uncooked egg remaining on top. Remove from broiler, fold over and serve.

Yield: 2 servings

Eggs Creole
Creole Sauce:

6 tablespoons oil
2 medium-sized onions, coarsely-chopped
2 cloves garlic, finely-minced
1 cup celery, coarsely-chopped
1 sweet red pepper, diced
1 pint fresh mushrooms, sliced
4 cups stewed tomatoes
½ cup okra, thinly-sliced
1 bay leaf
2 cups water
1 teaspoon salt
2 teaspoons chili powder
dash cayenne pepper
1 tablespoon arrowroot dissolved in a little water

*   *   *   *   *   *   *

9 hard-boiled eggs, cut into quarters
3 cups cooked rice (1 cup uncooked rice)

Heat oil in a large pot. Add onions, and garlic. Saute till lightly-browned. Add celery, pepper, and mushrooms. Sauté 5 minutes. Add tomatoes, okra, bay leaf, water, spices and arrowroot. Simmer for 15 minutes. In a large serving dish, lay quartered eggs over rice and ladle sauce over all.

Yield: 6 servings

Scramies and Cream Cheese

4 eggs
2 tablespoons milk (optional)
¼ cup grated onion
4 ounces cream cheese
  salt and pepper to taste
1 tomato, sliced

In a small mixing bowl, beat eggs with milk.
Heat grated onion in oiled skillet. Cut cream
cheese into small cubes. Pour eggs into skillet
and stir constantly with a wooden spoon.
When eggs are almost done, add cream cheese
and let it melt halfway into the eggs. Add salt
and pepper to taste. Serve with sliced tomatoes.

Yield: 2 servings

Pancakes

Pancakes provide you with the opportunity to
experiment with different grains, nuts and
seeds. This often results in amazing and delicious tastes and textures. Top pancakes with
fresh fruit, yogurt, honey butter, fruit butter,
grated fruit, or preserves.
Pancakes should be cooked on a moderately hot
griddle, lightly greased if necessary. Cook pancake until it has many bubbles on top and is
lightly-browned on the bottom. Then turn it
over and brown it on the other side.

Hint: Don't mix the batter *too* much. It should
be slightly lumpy. Only turn pancakes 1 time
on griddle.

Buckwheat Cakes

2 cups milk
2 eggs, beaten
2 tablespoons oil
1 tablespoon molasses
2 tablespoons honey
1½ teaspoons *Baking Powder* (see index)
½ teaspoon salt
· 1½ cups buckwheat flour

In a large mixing bowl, mix all the liquid ingredients. Stir in baking powder, salt and buckwheat flour. If batter is too runny add a little more flour. Cook on hot griddle.

Variation: Add 1 cup berries, such as blackberries, to batter.

Yield: 10-12 cakes

Fresh Corn Cakes

2 ears fresh corn (cut off cob)
¼ cup oil (peanut is nice)
3 tablespoons honey
2 eggs
1½ cups whole wheat flour
½ cup Indian meal (or cornmeal)
2½ teaspoons *Baking Powder* (see index)
1 teaspoon salt
milk

Mix the corn, oil, honey and eggs in a mixing bowl. Add dry ingredients and enough milk to make a lumpy batter. Cook on hot griddle.

Yield: 10-12 cakes

Potato Pancakes

3 medium-sized potatoes
2 tablespoons wheat germ
1 egg, beaten
grated onion
salt and pepper to taste
paprika

Grate raw potatoes with skins into a mixing
bowl. Add wheat germ and egg. Add grated
onion and salt and pepper to taste. Drop by
tablespoons on hot griddle and flatten with a
fork. Sprinkle with paprika.

Yield: 6 servings

Lucy's Whole Wheat Pancake and Banana Sandwich

2 cups whole wheat flour
1 tablespoon *Baking Powder* (see index)
1 teaspoon salt
1 tablespoon oil
1 egg, beaten
2 tablespoons honey
1½ cups milk or more if needed
3-4 bananas, ripe but firm

In a mixing bowl, mix flour, baking powder
and salt. Add oil, egg, honey and milk. Cook
on preheated griddle turning when bubbles
appear. Slice bananas lengthwise in quarters
and make a sandwich of pancake, then
banana, then pancake. Serve with honey.

Yield: 6 sandwiches

57

Banana-Sunflower Seed Pancakes

       3 cups whole wheat flour
       2 teaspoons salt
       1 tablespoon *Baking Powder* (see index)
       2 eggs
       2 tablespoons oil
       2 tablespoons honey
       2½ cups milk
       2 large bananas
       1 cup sunflower seeds

In a mixing bowl, mix first 3 ingredients. In separate bowl, beat eggs, then add oil, honey and milk. Add to dry mixture, using enough to make batter lumpy. Fold in sliced bananas and seeds. Go easy on the amount of batter put on the griddle.

Yield: approximately 15 cakes

Wheat-Corn Cakes

       2½ cups whole wheat flour
       1 cup cornmeal
       1 teaspoon salt
       1 tablespoon *Baking Powder* (see index)
       3 eggs, separated
       1 teaspoon honey
       ¾ cup oil
       2 cups milk (add more if needed)
       1 cup raisins (optional)

In a mixing bowl, mix dry ingredients. In a separate bowl, beat egg whites stiff. Set aside. Beat egg yolks with honey and add oil and milk. Add to dry ingredients with raisins. Fold in egg whites. Cook on hot griddle.

Yield: approximately 15 cakes

Rye Pancakes

2½ cups whole wheat flour
1 cup rye flour
½ teaspoon salt
1½ teaspoons *Baking Powder* (see index)
½ cup sesame seeds
2 eggs
2 cups milk
¼ cup honey
¼ cup oil

In a mixing bowl, mix dry ingredients. In separate bowl, beat eggs and milk, then add honey and oil. Add to the dry ingredients, just enough to make lumpy. If too thick add more milk. These pancakes take a little longer to cook than cakes usually do.

Yield: approximately 15 cakes

Soya-Raisin Griddle Cakes

1 cup whole wheat flour
½ cup soy flour
1 teaspoon salt
1½ teaspoons *Baking Powder* (see index)
1½ cups milk
1 egg, beaten
2 teaspoons molasses
1 tablespoon oil
1 tablespoon honey
1 cup raisins

In a mixing bowl, mix dry ingredients. In separate bowl, mix milk, egg, molasses, oil, honey and raisins. Add to dry ingredients and toss lightly for lumpy batter. Cook on hot, well-greased griddle. Yield: 10-12 cakes

59

Pecan Cakes

1½ cups milk
4 tablespoons oil
1 egg, beaten
3 tablespoons honey
1 tablespoon molasses
2 cups whole wheat flour
¼ cup wheat germ
1 tablespoon *Baking Powder* (see index)
½ teaspoon salt
1 cup pecans

Mix milk, oil, egg, honey and molasses in a mixing bowl. Stir in flour, wheat germ, baking powder, salt and ⅔ cup of the pecans. Reserve the other ⅓ cup of pecans to sprinkle on top of the cakes. Cook on hot griddle.

Variation: Substitute ½ cup cornmeal for an equal part of the flour. Substitute almonds or cashews for pecans.

Yield: approximately 12 cakes

Chapter 4

Our Daily Bread

Notes on Bread Baking

a) Keep whole grain and unbleached flours refrigerated.

b) Remember whole grains contain magnesium, potassium, silicon, copper, phosphorus, calcium, and B vitamins.

c) Grinding your own flour makes a tastier, more nutritious, and economical product, but it produces a heavier bread, so allow three risings.

d) Store flour in airtight containers.

e) Gluten retains air in the dough which makes it possible for dough to expand without exploding. Therefore a high-gluten content is valuable. Whole wheat flour has a high-gluten content.

f) Brewer's yeast is rich in the B vitamins and contains some protein and minerals, too. Replace 1 tablespoon of flour with 1 tablespoon of brewer's yeast.

g) Rice polish adds iron, phosphorus, calcium and protein. Replace ½ cup flour with ½ cup rice polish.

h) Wheat germ is one of the best sources of vitamin E. Replace anywhere from 1 tablespoon to 1 cup of flour with wheat germ.

General Guidelines to Making Bread

Read through this once or twice before beginning if this is your first time making bread. Refer to recipes for proportions.

Step 1

to dissolve yeast

a) Pour scalding milk or boiling water over honey to dissolve it.

b) Cool liquid to lukewarm—110°.

c) Sprinkle yeast in and stir.

d) Let it set 5 minutes till it has a light, spongy texture.

Note: The temperature of the liquid, Step "b," is most important. If the liquid is too hot, it will destroy the yeast; but if it is too cold, it will not activate the yeast.

If the yeast clumps together or doesn't sponge, the liquid temperature was not correct. *START AGAIN!*

Step 2

Add oil, salt and ½ of the flour.

Step 3

Beat mixture with wooden spoon, 100 strokes.

Step 4

Add the remaining flour.

Note: When dough is stirred enough, it will come away from the sides of the bowl.

Step 5

Turn dough out on lightly-floured board.

Step 6

With the palms of your hands pushing away from you, push the edges of the dough to the center as you knead. Knead until the dough has an elastic texture. It should be possible to make a print in the dough with your palm without having the dough stick to your hands.

Step 7

Rinse a big mixing bowl with warm water. Dry and lightly oil it. Shape dough into a ball and place it in the bowl.

Step 8

Lightly oil the surface of dough.

Step 9

Cover bowl with a warm, slightly-damp cloth, and set it in a warm place (about 85°). Be sure there are no drafts.

Step 10

Let dough rise until it is doubled in bulk, (about 1-2 hours).

Step 11

Punch dough down, letting air escape and giving fresh air to yeast. Let dough rise a second time, and punch it down when it is doubled.

Step 12

Optional third rising.

Step 13 ,

Shape dough into loaves. If two loaves are being made divide dough in half first. With a rolling pin, roll each piece into a rectangle ½ to ¾-inch thick, then roll up from narrow end into loaf shape. For a braided loaf, divide dough into three portions and roll each piece between your hands until the dough is long and thin. Then braid and work ends together with fingers.

Step 14

Place loaves in buttered loaf pans. The dough tends to stick more if oil is used.

Step 15

Cover pans with warm damp cloths.

Step 16

Let loaves rise in pans 20 to 30 minutes. Preheat oven to temperature called for in recipe (make allowances for your own oven).

Optional for browner crust: Beat an egg yolk with a little water, or just use a beaten egg white, and spread a coating over dough before putting in the oven. If adding sesame, poppy or caraway seeds on top, this will help them stick.

Step 17

Bake loaves until crusts are browned and bread has pulled away from sides of pans.

Step 18

Remove loaves from pans immediately. Set the bread on racks to cool.

Step 19

Cover loaves with a towel to keep warm till serving.

Note: Be sure bread is completely cool before storing in plastic bags, or it will become moist and soggy.

Functions of Bread Baking Ingredients

Ingredient	Type of Crust	Yeast Reaction	Other Functions
Water	Crisp	Yeast grows in it.	Potato water is good for rye or pumpernickel bread.
Milk	Brown	Scald it before using for best benefit to yeast.	Scalding prevents souring. Milk gives richer flavor than water.
Honey Molasses	Brown	It activates yeast.	Used as a sweetener. It makes bread moist.
Salt		Salt retards growth of yeast. Add it after yeast has sponged. It also balances yeast growth.	For flavor use about 1 teaspoon to 2 cups flour. Can be eliminated.
Eggs	Browner and thicker when spread on dough before placed in oven	None	They make a richer, tastier bread and crust. Use fertilized eggs whenever possible.
Oil Butter	Keeps crust smooth	To be added after yeast has sponged	They keep bread moist and more digestible.

Follow bread making guidelines for the following recipes, using these proportions:

Honey Wheat Bread (eggless)

3 cups warm water
¾ cup honey
1 tablespoon molasses
2 tablespoons yeast
¼ cup oil
1 teaspoon salt
5 cups whole wheat flour
3½ cups whole wheat flour or 2⅝ cups unbleached white flour and ⅞ cup wheat germ

Shape into 2 loaves and bake 50 to 60 minutes at 350°.

Yield: 2 loaves

Whole Wheat Bread (eggless)

2 cups warm water
⅓ cup honey
1 tablespoon molasses
1½ tablespoons yeast
2 tablespoons oil
2 teaspoons salt
3 cups whole wheat flour
3 cups whole wheat flour or 2¼ cups unbleached white flour and ¾ cup wheat germ

Shape into 2 loaves and bake 50 to 60 minutes at 350°.

Yield: 2 loaves

Rye Bread

2 tablespoons yeast
¼ cup warm water
⅓ cup molasses
1¾ cups milk (buttermilk preferably)
¼ cup oil
1½ teaspoons salt
4 tablespoons caraway seeds
3 cups rye flour
3 cups flour, whole wheat flour or 2¼ cups un-
    bleached white flour and ¾ cup wheat germ

Let dough rise 3 times. Then let it rise in the
pans 45 minutes. Bake 45 to 50 minutes at
325°.

Yield: 2 medium-sized loaves

Variation: Replace 1 tablespoon caraway
seed with 1 teaspoon anise seed.

Bran Bread

2¼ cups milk, scalded and cooled with
1 tablespoon butter
Add (after milk and butter have set 5 minutes)
½ cup warm water
⅓ cup honey
4 teaspoons yeast
1 cup bran
1 tablespoon brewer's yeast
2 cups whole wheat flour
2½ cups whole wheat flour or 1⅞ cups un-
    bleached white flour and ⅝ cup wheat
    germ

This requires only 1 rising and then a rising in the pan. Bake 45 minutes at 375°.

Yield: 1 good sized loaf

Swirl Bread

Prepare dough for *Whole Wheat Bread* (see index). After last rising, roll dough out flat with rolling pin. If making 2 loaves, divide the dough in half. Spread a generous layer of preserves on the surface leaving a 1½ inch margin of uncovered dough all the way around. Roll dough up like a jelly roll very carefully and slowly, so jelly doesn't ooze out of the ends. Pinch the sides together well. Bake as directed.

Yield: 1 or 2 loaves

Cinnamon-Raisin Swirl Bread

Prepare dough for *Whole Wheat Bread* (see index). After final rising, divide dough in half, roll out with a rolling pin into a ¾-inch thick rectangle. Spread a layer of honey on surface of the dough leaving a 1½-inch margin uncovered all the way around. Sprinkle cinnamon on honey (a little cloves or nutmeg may also be added). Spread 1 cup of raisins and 1 cup of pecans or walnuts across dough. Roll up like jelly rolls. Seal ends well and bake as directed.

Yield: 2 loaves

Wheat Germ Bread

2 cups warm water
⅓ cup honey
2 tablespoons yeast
1½ teaspoons salt
2 tablespoons oil
1 large egg, beaten
4 cups whole wheat flour
1 cup unbleached white flour
1½ cups wheat germ

Bake 50 minutes at 350°.

Yield: 2 medium-sized loaves

Hopi Indian Wheat Bread

1 cup warm water
1 cup milk, scalded and cooled
¼ cup honey
¼ cup molasses
2 tablespoons yeast
¼ cup oil
3 teaspoons salt
3 cups whole wheat flour, beaten 100 strokes
3 cups whole wheat flour or 2¼ cups un-
    bleached white flour and ¾ cup wheat germ
1 cup ground buckwheat groats
1 cup ground millet

Divide into 3 loaves and bake about 50 minutes at 350°.

Yield: 3 loaves

The following recipes for yeasted bread do not follow the general guidelines for bread baking:

Challah

2 tablespoons yeast
¼ cup honey
¼ cup warm water
4 cups whole wheat flour
3 cups unbleached white flour
1 cup wheat germ
1 tablespoon salt
3-4 eggs
2 tablespoons oil
2 cups water
1 egg yolk, beaten with a little butter or water
sprinkle of poppy seeds

In a small mixing bowl, dissolve yeast and honey in ¼ cup of water and let stand for 5 minutes.

Mix next 4 ingredients in a separate bowl. Make a well in the center and add the sponged yeast. Let stand 5 more minutes. Beat 100 strokes then mix in 3 to 4 eggs, oil and 2 cups of water.

Knead dough and let rise till double in bulk. Punch down and let rise again. Punch down again. Braid loaves and place in buttered pans. Let rise 30 minutes. Spread beaten egg yolk over dough. Sprinkle with poppy seeds. Bake about an hour at 375°.

Yield: 2 loaves

Anadama Bread
(made by early Massachusetts settlers)

- 1 cup boiling water
- ½ cup Indian meal or cornmeal
- 1 cup milk, scalded and cooled
- 2 tablespoons oil
- ¼ cup molasses
- ¼ cup honey
- 1 teaspoon salt
- 2 tablespoons yeast
- ½ cup warm water
- 1 teaspoon honey
- 6 cups flour (combination of whole wheat and unbleached is good)

In a mixing bowl, pour 1 cup boiling water over Indian meal to soften it. Add milk. Stir in oil, molasses, ¼ cup of honey, and salt. In a separate bowl, dissolve yeast in ½ cup of warm water and add 1 teaspoon of honey. Let stand for 5 minutes. Add meal mixture. Slowly add 6 cups of flour. Knead well. Cover and let rise till double in bulk then knead again. Divide dough into 2 portions and shape into loaves. Place in buttered pans and let rise 45 minutes. Bake 45 minutes at 375°.

English Soy Muffins

1 tablespoon honey
½ teaspoon molasses
1 tablespoon yeast
½ cup warm water
½ cup milk
¼ cup soy oil
1½ teaspoons salt
2 cups whole wheat flour
1 cup soy flour
cornmeal (for lining pan)

In a large mixing bowl, dissolve first the honey and molasses, then the yeast in warm water. Scald milk and let it cool. Add milk, oil and salt to yeast. Slowly add flour and turn dough out on floured board to knead. Place in a lightly-oiled bowl and let dough rise 1 hour. Punch down and knead again. Let it rise for another 30 minutes. Punch down and shape into muffins. Place on an ungreased cookie sheet sprinkled with cornmeal. Also sprinkle cornmeal on top of muffins. Let rise another hour. Bake about 10 minutes on each side till brown.

Yield: 10 large muffins

Butter Rolls

⅔ cup honey
2 tablespoons yeast
1 cup warm water
½ cup oil
3 eggs
2½ cups whole wheat flour
¾ cup wheat flour
⅓ cup milk
2 teaspoons salt

In a large mixing bowl, dissolve first the honey, then the yeast in water. Let stand 5 minutes. Add oil, eggs and whole wheat flour. Beat 100 strokes. Add wheat flour, milk and salt. Let dough rise till doubled in bulk. Stir it down in bowl and let rise again. Punch down. HANDLE DOUGH LIGHTLY. Roll out to ¼-inch thick and cut into rounds. Spread with 1-inch pieces of butter. Set rounds close together on cookie sheet and let them rise once more, till double. Bake 20 to 25 minutes at 350°.

Yield: approximately 2 dozen rolls

QUICK BREADS
muffins, biscuits, loaf breads

Berry Muffins
Preheat oven: 400°

1 cup whole wheat flour
¾ cup unbleached white flour
¼ cup wheat germ
½ teaspoon salt
1 tablespoon *Baking Powder* (see index)
⅓ cup honey
1 large egg
3 tablespoons oil
1 cup milk
1 cup berries

In a large mixing bowl, mix dry ingredients. Mix next 4 ingredients in separate bowl. Add enough of second mixture to dry ingredients to make a lumpy batter. Grease muffin cups and cover the bottom of them with a layer of berries or stir them into batter. Fill cups ½ to ¾ full with batter. Bake in preheated oven 20 to 25 minutes.

Yield: 14 muffins

Vanderploeg Apple Bread
Preheat oven: 350°

    3 tablespoons butter
    ¾ cup honey
    2 eggs
    1 teaspoon vanilla
    2 teaspoons *Baking Powder* (see index)
    5 tablespoons milk
    2 cups whole wheat pastry flour
    1 teaspoon salt
    2 cups chopped apples

In a medium-sized mixing bowl, cream honey and butter. Add eggs, vanilla and milk. In a large mixing bowl, mix baking powder with flour, salt and apple. Add butter mixture, mix well and bake in large, greased loaf pan in preheated oven for 1 hour.

Banana Bread
Preheat oven: 350°

    2½ cups whole wheat flour
    4 teaspoons *Baking Powder* (see index)
    1 teaspoon salt
    ¼ cup oil
    ¼ cup milk
    1 egg
    ½ cup honey
    3-4 very ripe bananas
    1 cup raisins
    1 cup nuts, chopped

In a large mixing bowl, mix first 3 ingredients. Blend oil, milk, egg, honey, and bananas in a blender. Add to dry ingredients. Mix in raisins and nuts. Turn into 1 large, greased loaf pan and bake about 55 minutes in a pre-heated oven.

Fig Muffins
Preheat oven: 400°

1 cup whole wheat flour
1 cup wheat germ
½ teaspoon salt
3 teaspoons *Baking Powder* (see index)
1 egg, beaten
¾ cup milk
⅓ cup honey (or part molasses)
2 tablespoons oil
¾ cup figs, chopped

In a large mixing bowl, mix dry ingredients. Add beaten egg, milk, honey and oil. In a small, heat-proof bowl, pour boiling water over figs and let stand 10 minutes. Drain and add to dough. Grease muffin cups and fill them ½ to ¾ full. Bake 20 to 25 minutes in a preheated oven.

Note: Batter for muffins is lumpy. Do not beat.

Yield: 14 muffins

Mrs. Vanderploeg's Health Bread
Preheat oven: 350°

½ cup honey
1 egg, beaten
¼ teaspoon salt
4 teaspoons *Baking Powder* (see index)
1 cup oats
1 cup graham flour
1 cup bran
1 cup raisins
1 cup milk

In a large mixing bowl, beat honey and egg together. Sift salt, baking powder, flour and add along with oats and bran to honey and egg. In a small saucepan, boil raisins in hot water till they puff up. Cool, drain and add. Stir in milk. Blend well. Turn batter into well-greased loaf pan. Bake 1 hour in preheated oven.

Pumpkin Bread
Preheat oven: 350°

1¾ cups whole wheat flour
3 teaspoons *Baking Powder* (see index)
¾ teaspoon salt
1 tablespoon cinnamon
1 tablespoon nutmeg
2 eggs, beaten
½ cup oil
⅓ cup water
1 cup pumpkin
¾ cup honey

In a large mixing bowl, mix flour, baking powder, salt, cinnamon and nutmeg. In a small mixing bowl, add eggs to oil. In a medium-sized mixing bowl, add water to pumpkin. Add eggs to pumpkin mixture and add honey, mixing well. Blend with dry ingredients. Bake in large, greased loaf pan in preheated oven for 1 hour and 15 minutes.

Herbed Biscuits
Preheat oven: 450°

1 cup whole wheat flour
9/16 cup unbleached white flour
3/16 cup wheat germ
1/4 cup dry milk powder
1 teaspoon salt
1/4 teaspoon basil
1/4 teaspoon marjoram
    dash garlic powder
1/4 cup butter or safflower oil or other oil
3/4 cup milk

In a large mixing bowl, mix first 8 ingredients. Cut in butter with fork or pastry blender. Add milk. Roll dough 1/4 to 1/2-inch thick. Shape into biscuits and bake on ungreased cookie sheet. Bake 12 to 15 minutes in a preheated oven.

Yield: 14 biscuits

Lucy's Cornbread
(Light and lovable) Preheat oven: 425°

  1 cup yellow cornmeal
  ¾ cup whole wheat flour
  4 teaspoons *Baking Powder* (see index)
  1 teaspoon salt
  1 egg
  3 tablespoons oil
  1 cup milk
  ¼ cup honey

Sift together, into a large mixing bowl, corn-meal, flour, baking powder and salt. Beat together egg, oil, milk and honey and mix with dry mixture. Fill a well-oiled 8-inch by 8-inch pan. Bake in preheated oven 20 to 25 minutes.

Spanish Corn Bread
Preheat oven: 275°

  1 cup buttermilk
  1 cup yellow cornmeal
  1 cup whole wheat flour
  3 teaspoons honey
  1 teaspoon salt
  1 teaspoon *Baking Powder* (see index)
  1 egg, beaten
  ¼ cup oil
  1 ear fresh corn, cut off cob and cooked until tender
  4 ounces green chilies, chopped
  4 ounces pimientos, chopped
  2 cups unprocessed cheese, grated

In a large mixing bowl, combine all the ingredients in the order given. Stir until well mixed. Pour into greased pan 13 inches by 9½ inches by 2 inches. Bake for 30 minutes.

Almond-Oat Muffins
Preheat oven: 375°

2 cups whole wheat flour
1½ cups oats
1 teaspoon salt
2½ teaspoons *Baking Powder* (see index)
1 cup non-fat dry milk powder
1 teaspoon cinnamon
1 teaspoon mace
½ cup sesame seeds
½ cup almonds, chopped
½ cup sunflower seeds
3 eggs, beaten
½ cup honey
¼ cup oil
1 teaspoon almond extract

In a large mixing bowl, mix dry ingredients, nuts and seeds. Combine liquids in a separate bowl. Then slowly add to dry ingredients. Keep adding liquid until batter is lumpy. Fill greased muffin cups ¾ full. Bake 20 to 30 minutes in preheated oven.

Yield: 14 biscuits

My Molasses Corn Bread
Preheat oven: 350°

> 2 eggs, beaten
> 1¾ cups milk
> ¼ cup honey
> ¼ cup molasses
> ½ cup oil
> 2 tablespoons *Baking Powder* (see index)
> 1 teaspoon salt
> 3 cups yellow cornmeal
> 1 cup whole wheat flour

In a large mixing bowl, mix eggs, milk, honey, molasses and oil. Add baking powder, salt, cornmeal and flour. Place in greased loaf pan and bake 50 to 60 minutes in a preheated oven.

Yield: 1 large loaf

Raisin Corn Bread
Preheat oven: 425°

> ¾ cups yellow cornmeal
> 1¾ cups unbleached white flour
> ¼ cup wheat germ
> 3 teaspoons *Baking Powder* (see index)
> ½ teaspoon salt
> 1 egg, beaten
> ¾ cup plus 1 tablespoon milk
> 2 tablespoons oil
> ⅛ cup honey
> ⅛ cup molasses
> ½ cup raisins
> sesame seeds

In a large mixing bowl, mix dry ingredients.
Then add egg, milk, oil, honey and molasses.
Mix in raisins. Pour into greased pan 8
inches by 8 inches. Sprinkle sesame seeds on
top. Bake in preheated oven for 20 minutes.

Orange-Sunflower Seed Biscuits
Preheat oven: 450°

2 cups whole wheat flour
3 teaspoons *Baking Powder* (see index)
½ teaspoon salt
¼ cup butter, oil, or safflower shortening
¾ cup milk
½ cup sunflower seeds (optional)
1 teaspoon grated orange peel

In a large mixing bowl, mix dry ingredients.
Cut in butter or oil with fork or pastry
blender. Add the milk to make a soft dough.
Stir in sunflower seeds and orange peel. Roll
out dough ½ to ¾-inch thick. Cut into
biscuit shapes. Bake 12 to 15 minutes on an
ungreased cookie sheet, in a preheated oven.

Yield: 14 biscuits

Cheese Sticks
Preheat oven: 400°

2 cups sharp cheddar cheese, grated
¼ pound butter, softened
1 cup whole wheat flour, sifted
¼ teaspoon salt
dash cayenne pepper
dash paprika

Cream the cheese and butter together until smooth. Sift the dry ingredients together, except the paprika, and add to the cheese mixture. Shape into a loaf and chill thoroughly. Cut into thin slices. Cut each slice into ½-inch wide sticks. Bake on lightly-greased cookie sheet in preheated oven for 20 minutes. Remove from oven and sprinkle with paprika. Leftovers may be stored in airtight containers. These are best when served hot.

Yield: 6 dozen sticks

UNYEASTED BREADS

Macrobiotic Bread

1½ cups unbleached white flour
½ cup wheat germ
3 cups whole wheat flour
1 cup buckwheat flour
2 teaspoons salt
2½-3 cups warm water
sesame seeds to sprinkle on top

In a large mixing bowl, mix flours, wheat germ and salt. Stir in water slowly enough to form a dough. Knead dough on a floured board. Immediately shape into 2 large or 3 small loaves and place in oiled pans. Sprinkle with sesame seeds. Bake approximately 1½ hours at 350°.

Variations: 1. Substitute for buckwheat flour: 1 cup rye flour or 1 cup potato flour or 1 cup rice flour. 2. Add any variety of nuts or seeds and herbs for added flavor and texture.

Chapatti
(flat bread similar to tortilla)

1 cup mixed grains or whole wheat flour
½ cup water
1 teaspoon salt

In a large mixing bowl, mix ingredients and knead well. Break off small portions and roll in little balls. Roll balls out flat and thin with a rolling pin. Cook in oiled, hot skillet or on griddle. Chapatti is cooked when brown spots appear. Cook on both sides. Eat plain, or with butter or honey. There are endless uses for this quick bread. See index for recipes using chapatti.

Yield: 5-6 chapatti

Sopaipillas
Indian flat bread

  2 cups whole wheat flour
  ½ teaspoon salt
  2 teaspoons *Baking Powder* (see index)
  1 tablespoon butter
  ¾ cup water (approximately)

In a large mixing bowl, mix flour, salt, and baking powder. Work in butter with fingers till pea-sized balls form. Add water to make soft dough (not sticky). Form into round balls about the size of golf balls. Flatten with the palms of your hands to about ¼-inch thick. Fry in deep oil. They will puff up. Serve with honey.

Yield: approximately 3½ dozen

Chapter 5

Drink Up

Beverages

A nourishing drink can round out a meal, be a meal by itself, or serve as a refreshing, in-between-meals snack. A blender is an invaluable aid in preparing beverages. It will help dissolve the honey used in most of these recipes and will mix the ingredients to a perfect blend. A juicer is also helpful in making fresh fruit and vegetable juices.

Banana Smoothie

4 medium-sized bananas
½ cup water (approximately)
1 tablespoon honey

Peel bananas, wrap them in a plastic bag and set them in a freezer overnight. The next day, put enough water in a blender to cover the tips of the blades. Add honey and blend. Then slice ⅔ of a frozen banana. Add banana slices to honey and water. Blend until smooth. Slice the remaining bananas, add them slowly and blend till smooth. This drink should be thick enough to eat with a spoon.

Variations:
1. add 1 teaspoon peanut butter with the water and honey
2. add 6 dates with the ⅔ of a sliced banana
3. add 1 teaspoon carob powder with the honey and water
4. use only 2 bananas and add milk to make a thinner shake
5. use 3 cups of frozen strawberries instead of bananas
6. try any frozen fruit to replace bananas

Yield: 2 servings

Banana-Coconut Milk

1 tablespoon honey
¾ cup coconut milk
3 frozen bananas, sliced
4 dates pitted (optional)

Blend honey and coconut milk. Slowly add bananas and blend. Add dates and blend until smooth.

Yield: 4 servings

Banana Shake

1 cup milk (can use coconut milk)
3 tablespoons honey
½ cup dates, pitted
1 cup mashed bananas
1 cup yogurt
½ teaspoon vanilla

Blend milk, honey and dates. Add bananas, yogurt and vanilla and blend briefly.

Yield: 3 servings

Orange-Banana Juice

3 cups orange juice
2 medium-sized ripe bananas

Blend till smooth.

Yield: 4 servings

Orange Juice Cocktail

2 cups orange juice, unsweetened
1 egg, raw
1 small banana, mashed
1 tablespoon Tiger's milk
1 teaspoon wheat germ

Combine all ingredients in a blender. Blend
until smooth.

Yield: 2 servings

Lemonade or Limeade for One

1 glass water
juice of 1 lemon or lime
honey to taste
fresh mint

Combine first 3 ingredients in a blender and
blend well. Limeade requires a little more
sweetener. Add ice cubes and serve with
fresh mint.

Yogurt-Fruit Shakes

¼ cup yogurt
¼ cup fresh fruit
3 tablespoons honey
1¾ cups yogurt

Combine ¼ cup of yogurt, fruit and honey in blender and blend until smooth. Add 1¾ cups of yogurt and blend briefly, until mixed. Add more honey if sweeter taste is desired. I recommend pineapple or peaches for this drink.

Yield: 2 servings

Carrot-Yogurt Drink

1 medium-sized carrot, grated
⅓ cup yogurt
2 tablespoons honey
1 cup yogurt

Place carrot, ⅓ cup of yogurt and honey in a blender. Blend until smooth. Add 1 cup of yogurt and blend briefly, until mixed. Good breakfast drink.

Yield: 2 servings

Meditator's Mix

2 cups carrot juice
1 pint vanilla ice cream
1 teaspoon almond extract

Combine all ingredients in a blender and blend until smooth.

Yield: 4 servings

Carrot-Apple Drink

1½ cups carrot juice
½ cup apple juice
1 teaspoon honey
dash cloves

Combine all ingredients in a blender and blend until smooth.

Yield: 2 servings

Pero Delight for One

1 cup boiling water
1 teaspoon pero
2 teaspoons honey
1 tablespoon milk or cream
1 teaspoon vanilla

Pour boiling water over pero and honey. Add milk and vanilla. This drink has a taste similar to coffee ice cream.

Note: Pero is a rye and barley grain beverage, a coffee substitute. It is available at most health food stores.

Apple-Fenugreek Shake

1 banana, sliced
1½ cups milk
1 cup apple juice
½ cup cold fenugreek tea

Combine all ingredients in blender and blend until smooth.

Yield: 3 servings

Fenugreek-Carob Shake

8 ounces milk
2 tablespoons carob
½ cup cold fenugreek tea
2 bananas, sliced

In a blender, blend milk, carob, and tea. Slowly add bananas, and blend till smooth.

Yield: 4-6 servings

Carob Milk

3 tablespoons carob powder
3 tablespoons honey
2 cups milk
2 cups crushed ice

In a blender, blend all ingredients. Add more honey if a sweeter taste is desired. Always blend carob powder in blender to dissolve it.

Yield: 4 servings

Sumac Drink

2 cups sumac tea, cold
1 teaspoon lemon juice
⅓ cup honey

In a blender, blend ingredients briefly. Add more honey if desired. Good summertime drink.

Yield: 2 servings

Vegetable Cooler

3 cups carrot juice
⅓ cup celery juice
⅓ cup spinach juice

In a blender, blend ingredients and serve with a sprig of parsley.

Yield: 4 servings

Chapter 6

Sizzling Soups 'n' Sandwiches

Notes on Soup Stock, Thickening, Seasonings

1. Use water from cooked or steamed vegetables for stock base.

2. Save water that beans have soaked in to use as stock for bean soup. This makes the stock rich in minerals.

3. Use about 2 tablespoons of barley or rice to thicken soup.

4. Before making soup, melt 2 tablespoons of butter in soup pot. Stir in 2 tablespoons of flour and make a paste. Then slowly add stock. This will act as a thickening agent.

Note: Buckwheat, potato, or brown rice flour is good for this.

5. Do not save water from broccoli or cabbage as their flavors are too strong for a mild soup.

6. Don't go overboard on seasonings. Let the natural flavor of your vegetables come through.

7. Add herbs to soup when it is nearly done so that the herbs retain their flavor.

8. Onions or mushrooms may be sauteed before they are added to soups.

9. When salting soup, use 1 teaspoon salt to 1 quart water.

10. If soup gets too salty, add some raw potatoes for 10 to 15 minutes. They will absorb the salt.

Russian Cabbage Borscht

3-4 medium-sized onions, chopped
2-3 cloves garlic, chopped
10-20 tomatoes, cut into small pieces
10 potatoes, sliced with skins
6 carrots, sliced
2 bay leaves
dash thyme
3-4 heads cabbage, shredded
salt to taste
cayenne pepper to taste
1 cup honey
juice of 3 lemons

Boil onions and garlic in a large pot half full of water. Add tomatoes, potatoes and carrots and simmer, covered, for 1 hour. Add next 3 ingredients. Cover and simmer another hour. Cabbage will cook down. Add salt and pepper to taste.

Add honey and lemon juice and simmer another half hour.

Yield: 1 big pot of soup

Cream of Cauliflower Soup

3 tablespoons butter
½ small onion, chopped
3 tablespoons whole wheat flour
3 cups milk
1 head cauliflower, broken into flowerets
   salt and cayenne pepper to taste
   few sprigs parsley

In a large pot, melt butter and add onion. Cook a few minutes. Add flour and stir to make a paste. Slowly add milk allowing it to thicken. Add cauliflower and simmer about 30 minutes. Add salt and cayenne pepper to taste and serve with parsley.

Yield: 6 servings

Gazpacho (cold Spanish soup)

4 tomatoes, cut into small pieces
1 green pepper, chopped
1 onion, chopped
1 cucumber, chopped
2 cups tomato juice
1½ cloves garlic, crushed
1 tablespoon parsley
3 tablespoons oil (preferably olive)
3 tablespoons wine or cider vinegar
   salt and cayenne pepper to taste
10 pitted, black olives (optional)

In a large bowl, mix all the ingredients, except the olives. Blend half of the mixture in the blender. Add to the other half of the mixture. Add olives. Serve with croutons.

Yield: 6 servings

Lentil Soup

2 cups lentils, soaked overnight
8 cups water or stock
1 large onion, sliced
1 clove garlic, chopped
2 tablespoons oil
½ cup celery, sliced
2 carrots, sliced thin
1 bay leaf
2 tablespoons Tamari soy sauce

In a large pot, simmer lentils in water or stock for 30 minutes. In a skillet, sauté onion and garlic in oil. Add to soup. Simmer for 1 hour. Add celery, carrots, bay leaf and soy sauce last 30 minutes of cooking. If soup is too thick, add a little bit of water.

Yield: 10 servings

Lima Bean Soup

2 cups lima beans, soaked overnight
4½ cups stock
1 carrot, sliced
½ cup celery, sliced
½ onion, sliced
  bay leaf
  salt to taste

In a large pot, cook beans in stock. When stock begins to thicken add vegetables and seasonings. If soup is too thick, thin it with a little water. Cook until vegetables are tender.

Yield: 6 servings

Mushroom Kreplach Soup

Dough for Kreplach noodles

1½ cups wheat flour *or* ¾ cup unbleached
  white flour and ¾ cup soy flour *or* 1⅛ cups
  unbleached white flour and ⅜ cup wheat
  germ
½ teaspoon salt
2 eggs

Sift flour and salt on to a board. Make a well
in the center of the flour. Break the eggs into
the well and beat them into the flour with a
wooden spoon. Add a little water if necessary to form a dough. Knead on a floured
board until smooth.

Filling

1 cup mushrooms, chopped into small pieces
2 tablespoons oil
2 eggs, hard boiled, chopped
1 teaspoon minced onion
  salt to taste
  pinch of cayenne pepper

In a skillet, sauté mushrooms in oil. Mix
with eggs, onion, salt and pepper.
Roll dough out on lightly-floured board. Cut
into 1½-inch squares. Fill each center with
½ teaspoon of filling. Fold square over to
form a triangle. Pinch sides together. Drop
into boiling, salted water till Kreplachs rise
to the top. Serve in clear soup, broth, or with
tomato sauce.

Yield: about 30 Kreplachs

Simple Onion Soup

4 onions, sliced in rings
oil
5 cups stock
1 teaspoon Tamari soy sauce
salt and cayenne pepper to taste
5-6 slices whole wheat toast or 2 cups croutons
½ cup milk or cream (optional)
sharp cheese, grated to sprinkle on soup

In a skillet, sauté onion rings in oil till they are lightly-browned. Put stock in a large pot. Add onion rings to stock and simmer for 30 minutes. Add soy sauce, salt and cayenne. Place a slice of whole wheat toast on the bottom of each bowl and pour soup over the top, or use croutons on the top of the soup. Add milk or cream for thicker soup and top with grated cheese.

Variation: Add a grated carrot.

Yield: 5-6 servings

Sweet Sue's Potato Soup

1 large onion, sliced
2 tablespoons oil
7 large potatoes
1 quart water
1 quart milk
2 teaspoons salt
cayenne pepper to taste

In a skillet, sauté onion in oil. Drain. Dice potatoes into a large pot and add water along with onion. Cover and boil gently for 15 minutes, or until potatoes are tender. Mash potatoes without draining them. Add milk, salt, cayenne pepper and heat slowly, stirring to prevent sticking.

Yield: 8 servings

Cream of Tomato Soup

4 cups tomatoes, cubed
½ cup milk
2 tablespoons butter
½ cup onions or chives, chopped
2 tablespoons whole wheat flour
1 cup milk
  salt to taste
¼ teaspoon curry powder
½ teaspoon oregano

Puree tomatoes with ½ cup of milk in blender until very smooth. Melt 2 tablespoons of butter in a soup pot. Add the chopped onions or chives and cook for a minute. Add 2 tablespoons of flour and stir into a paste. Slowly add 1 cup of milk. When thickened add tomato puree, salt, curry powder and oregano. Simmer 30 to 45 minutes.

Yield: 6 servings

Sandwiches and Spreads

When serving sandwiches use homemade bread, chappati, or commercial bread marked "no preservatives added."

When using mayonnaise try making your own or buy soy or safflower style. Most other kinds of mayonnaise are loaded with preservatives and additives.

Summer Sandwich

       cucumber slices
       romaine lettuce
       tomato slices
       chives
       salt to taste
       sour cream

Layer the cucumber, lettuce, tomato and chives on a slice of bread. Salt to taste. Top with sour cream. Serve with *Cream of Tomato Soup* (see index).

Alfalfa Sprout Sandwich

       lettuce
       tomato slices
       green onion, chopped (use tops)
       alfalfa sprouts
       mayonnaise

Layer ingredients on bread in the order listed. Try this sandwich with *Simple Onion Soup* (see index).

Guacamole Spread

1 ripe avocado, mashed
1 tablespoon mayonnaise or yogurt
1 squeeze of lemon juice
  dash Tamari soy sauce (optional)
1 green onion, chopped
1 rib celery, chopped

Blend all ingredients with a fork. Excellent on *Chappati* (see index).

Yield: approximately 1 cup

Avocado Sandwich

romaine lettuce
avocado, sliced or *Guacamole Spread* (see above)
tomato slices
raw mushrooms, thinly-sliced

Layer ingredients on bread in the order listed. Cashews can be a nice addition to avocado spreads or sandwiches.

Carrot-Apple-Raisin Sandwich

1 small carrot, grated
1 small apple, grated
1 tablespoon raisins
1 teaspoon nuts, chopped (optional)
1 tablespoon mayonnaise

Combine all the ingredients and spread on bread. Serve with *Cream of Tomato Soup* (see index).
Hint: pumpernickel bread could make this a real treat.

Cheese Fingers

30 slices wheat germ bread, sliced thin
¼ pound butter
½ pound soft yellow cheese
1 cup *Barbecue Sauce* (see index)
1 teaspoon honey

Remove crusts from bread. Roll each slice of bread out flat with a rolling pin. Mix butter, cheese, barbecue sauce and honey together in a mixer until well-blended. Spread mixture over bread, but not too thickly. Roll each slice like a jelly roll. Place on a cookie sheet, cover with foil and freeze. When ready to serve, partially defrost. Remove foil. Place under broiler. Brown on one side. Turn them over and brown on the other side. Serve piping hot.

Yield: 30 sandwiches

Broiled Cheese Deluxe Sandwich

raw mushrooms, sliced
onions, sliced in rings and separated
tomato slices
cheese slices
sesame seeds

Lay first 4 ingredients on a slice of bread in the order given. Slip under broiler until cheese melts. Top with sesame seeds.
Try this with *Simple Onion* or *Cream of Cauliflower Soup* (see index).

Chick Pea Spread

1 pound chick peas, cooked tender
4 cloves garlic, well-crushed
4 teaspoons tahini (sesame seed butter available
at health food stores or grocery stores with
health food sections)
½ bell pepper
1 tablespoon lemon juice
salt to taste

Mash all ingredients together and spread.
Try as a spread for celery.

Yield: 6 sandwiches

Grandma's Eggplant Spread

1 medium-sized eggplant
1 small onion, finely-chopped
2 tablespoons olive oil
1 clove garlic, crushed
¼ cup green pepper, diced
½ cup cucumber, chopped
salt and pepper to taste

Place whole eggplant on a broiler pan. Broil
for about 10 minutes turning the eggplant
until the outer shell browns and splits. Remove the peeling carefully after the eggplant
has cooled. Mash the inside with a fork or
place it in a blender and blend till eggplant
is smooth. Combine with the rest of the ingredients. Mash until spreadable. Chill
thoroughly. Serve with rye or any other
whole grain bread.

Yield: 6 servings

Grilled Blue Cheese and Asparagus Sandwich

    mayonnaise
    tomato slices
    asparagus spears, gently cooked
    squeeze of lemon juice
    blue cheese

On one side of bread, spread a layer of mayonnaise, then put tomatoes, then asparagus. Squeeze lemon on asparagus. Crumble or grate blue cheese on top. Grill.

Serve with *Cream of Tomato or Simple Onion Soup* (see index).

Date-Fig Spread

    6 dates
    6 figs
    2 almonds
    enough carrot juice, or other juice, to thin out.

In a blender, blend all ingredients till smooth. Very good on *Chappati* (see index), or as an addition to peanut butter sandwiches.

                Yield: approximately 3 sandwiches

Yogurt and Fig Spread

Boil figs for a few minutes (save juice for other cooking). Remove stems and blend till smooth. Add a little fig or apple juice (if needed to thin out).

Spread yogurt on bread and top with Fig Spread.

Peanut Butter Delights
(try making your own peanut butter)

1) Old-Fashioned Peanut Butter (see index)
   honey
   banana slices
   sunflower seeds (optional)
   lettuce

Note: Lettuce sounds like a strange addition, but it is really very tasty on a peanut butter sandwich. Its moistness helps you chew and digest the peanut butter.

2) Old-Fashioned Peanut Butter (see index)
   dates or figs, sliced
   banana slices (optional)

3) Old-Fashioned Peanut Butter (see index)
   Crab-Apple Apple Butter (see index)
   raisins

4) Old-Fashioned Peanut Butter (see index)
   Peach Butter (see index)
   Peach slices

Spread a thin layer of peanut butter on a slice of bread. Add other ingredients in order listed.

Sliced Egg and Onion Sandwich

hard boiled eggs, sliced
chives or onion, chopped
salt and dash cayenne pepper to taste
pinch of dried tarragon
raw mushrooms, sliced
few sprigs parsley
mayonnaise

Layer ingredients on bread in the order listed. With a small bowl of *Lentil Soup* (see index), this could be a hearty meal.

Chapter 7

Well-Dressed Salads

Salads and Dressings

A good salad is enhanced by a colorful and attractive presentation. Take time to prepare vegetables, and remember to add tomatoes last. Top a salad with sprouts, nuts, seeds, wheat germ, or grated cheese to round it out.

Hint: Let each person dress the salad to his own taste.

Carrot-Pineapple-Raisin Salad

2 carrots, grated on small end of grater
1 apple, grated
½ small, fresh pineapple, cut into small chunks
½ cup raisins
    dash cinnamon
1 tablespoon plain yogurt to moisten

Mix all ingredients and serve. This is a very refreshing summer salad, or good addition to a rice dinner.

Yield: 4 servings

Artichoke Heart and Cauliflower Salad

    1 head romaine lettuce
    8 artichoke hearts
    8 cauliflowerets, sliced thin
    ½ cup almonds, slivered

Make individual salads by arranging, on a bed of romaine lettuce, 2 of the artichoke hearts, 2 cauliflowerets, and ⅛ cup of almonds. Cover with *Garlic Dressing, French,* or *Lemon Dressing* (see index).

Yield: 4 servings

Marinated Cold Bean Salad

    1 cup green beans, steamed
    1 cup red kidney beans, cooked
    1 cucumber, sliced
    1 tablespoon oil
    3 tablespoons vinegar (red wine)
    1 teaspoon honey
    oregano to taste
    dash garlic salt

Mix first 3 ingredients in a serving dish. In a separate bowl, mix remaining ingredients. Blend well. Cover bean mixture with the marinade and chill till serving.

Yield: 6, ½-cup servings

Beet Salad

1½ cups raw beets, shredded
¾ cup pineapple chunks
⅓ cup honey
2 tablespoons lemon juice
dash salt

Mix beets and pineapple together. In a separate bowl mix together the honey, lemon juice and salt and serve over beets and pineapple.

Yield: 3 servings

Country Coleslaw

½ head red cabbage, shredded
½ head green cabbage, shredded
½ cup carrots, diced
½ cup raisins
2 tablespoons onion, finely-chopped
2 teaspoons salt
dash cayenne pepper
2 tablespoons caraway seeds
1 tablespoon celery seeds
1-2 tablespoons apple cider vinegar
1 tablespoon honey
mayonnaise

Mix all ingredients and add enough mayonnaise (homemade, soy or safflower) to make coleslaw creamy. Chill well before serving.

Variations: Add 1 cup sprouts, use yogurt instead of mayonnaise, or add some dill seed.

Yield: 6 servings

111

Persian Salad

    1 cucumber, sliced
    ½ cup raisins
    4 radishes, sliced
    ⅛ teaspoon salt
    ½ cup plain yogurt
    ½ teaspoon mint, crushed

> Arrange the cucumber, raisins, and radishes in a bowl in layers. Sprinkle salt on top of this. Blend yogurt with mint and pour over top of salad.

Yield: 2 servings

Chinese Cukes

    2-3 firm cucumbers
    ¼ teaspoon salt
    ½ cup vinegar
    ½ cup water
    1 tablespoon dill weed
    ⅛ teaspoon white pepper
    1 inch cube fresh ginger, diced, or 1 teaspoon ginger powder

> Slice cucumbers paper thin. Blend the remaining ingredients with a fork. Pour over cucumbers and marinate in the refrigerator until well chilled. Zucchini squash may be substituted for cucumbers.

Yield: 4 servings

Garden Supreme Salad

1 head leafy lettuce
1 carrot, diced
1 head red cabbage, shredded
1 cup raw peas
2 green onions, sliced including stems
2 flowerets raw cauliflower, sliced
1 tomato, wedged
1 zucchini or cucumber, sliced
   sprouts on top

Toss lightly and serve with *Yogurt-Caraway Dressing* or *Thousand Island Dressing* (see index).

Yield: 6 servings

Spinach Salad

1 pound raw spinach, broken into bite-sized pieces
¼ cup leeks or chives, chopped
2 white radishes, sliced (optional)
10 raw mushrooms, sliced thin
1 carrot, cut in long thin strips with a paring knife

Toss lightly with *French Dressing* (see index) and serve.

Yield: 3-4 servings

Tabulee Assyrian Style Salad

    1 cup cracked wheat
  10 tomatoes, finely-chopped, seeds removed
    2 cucumbers, finely-chopped
    1 bell pepper, finely-chopped
    1 bunch green onions, finely chopped
  1½ ounces olive oil
  ½ cup fresh lemon juice
    salt and pepper to taste
    lettuce leaves
    cabbage leaves
    avocado slices

Cover the cracked wheat with water. Remove wheat a handful at a time squeezing out the water between your palms. Place it in a bowl and let it stand for 3 hours. It will still be a little moist after you have squeezed the water out. Add the tomatoes, cucumbers, pepper and onions. Add oil, lemon juice, salt and pepper. Stir all together and serve on a bed of lettuce and cabbage. Top with avocado slices.

Variation: Add fresh or dried mint, or radishes.

Yield: 6-8 servings

Stuffed Tomato with Avocado Spread

Wash whole tomato and cut out inside leaving ¼ inch to the skin. Mix the pulp with *Guacamole Spread* (see index) and stuff tomato. Split sides at top of tomato and partially open for a more attractive serving.

Lucy's Marinated Vegetable Salad

2 cups beets, sliced
2 cups green beans, cut
1 medium-sized cucumber, sliced
1 red onion, sliced into thin rings
1 small head cauliflower (buds only)
1 green pepper, cut in rings
   Oil and Vinegar Dressing (see index)

Steam vegetables till barely tender. Remove
vegetables from heat, cover with oil and vinegar dressing, and marinate in the refrigerator,
in covered pan, for several hours. Remove
occasionally, drain marinade and rebaste
vegetables. Serve on a bed of leafy lettuce.

Hint: A sliced, hard-boiled egg served on top
adds a nice touch.

Yield: 6 servings

Steamed Vegetable Salad

Use amounts desired:

cauliflower flowerets
string beans
asparagus tips
chives, chopped
salt to taste
dash tarragon

Steam vegetables, then add chives, salt and
tarragon. Serve over bed of lettuce with *Oil and
Vinegar Dressing* (see index) or just add a few
squeezes of lemon juice.

115

Egg Salad

- 2 eggs, hard- or medium-boiled
- 4 tablespoons mayonnaise or yogurt
- 3 tablespoons onion, chopped
- 1 teaspoon prepared mustard
- 1 teaspoon salt
- 1 rib celery, chopped
- dash cayenne pepper
- dash tarragon

Mash eggs, and add the rest of the ingredients. Serve over lettuce with tomato wedges. Top with sprouts.

Yield: ¾ cup

Macaroni Salad

- 2 cups wheat soy macaroni, cooked
- ½ cup carrots, shredded
- ⅓ cup green pepper, chopped
- ½ cup celery, chopped
- ⅓ cup onion, finely-chopped
- ⅛ teaspoon garlic powder
- 3 hard-boiled eggs, chopped (optional)
- ½-¾ cup mayonnaise (homemade, soy or safflower)
- 1 teaspoon salt
- dash cayenne pepper
- parsley sprigs

Mix all the ingredients and keep refrigerated till serving. Add sprouts if desired. Top with parsley sprigs.

Yield: 4-6 servings

Potato Salad

8 medium-sized potatoes
½ onion, chopped
1 cup celery, diced
½ cup carrots, shredded (optional)
3 hard-boiled eggs, sliced or chopped (optional)
  Oil and Vinegar Dressing (see index)
1 cup or more mayonnaise (homemade, soy or
    safflower)

Cook potatoes with the skins till tender.
Cool and cut into cubes. Add onion, celery,
carrots, hard-boiled eggs, and oil and vinegar
dressing. Stir in the mayonnaise. Add more
if salad is too dry.

Variation: Add ½ cup alfalfa sprouts, garlic
powder or dill seed.

Yield: 8-12 servings

Sweet Summer Fiesta Salad

3 cups fresh fruit
½ cup nuts or seeds
½ cup raisins
⅓ to ½ cup honey (depending on how sweet
        the fruit is)
1 teaspoon vanilla
  cinnamon to taste

Toss fresh fruit, nuts or seeds, and raisins.
Add honey and vanilla and stir well to coat
all the fruit. Add cinnamon to taste. Eat
plain, with yogurt, or serve over cake.

Yield: 4-5 servings

117

Springtime Salad

few lettuce leaves
watermelon chunks, seeds removed
apple chunks, seeds removed
scoop cottage cheese
4 thin orange slices

Place leaves of leafy lettuce on bottom of salad bowl. Cover with watermelon and apple chunks. Top with cottage cheese in the center and arrange orange slices around it.

Yield: 1 serving

Nutty Fruit Salad

3 bananas, ripe but still firm, sliced
½ cup figs, sliced with stems removed
½ cup dates, pitted and sliced
¼ cup almonds
¼ cup pecans

Mix ingredients together. This is a good lunch by itself or goes well with a rice dinner. May use ½ cup of other type of nut if almonds and pecans are not available. Serve plain or with yogurt.

Yield: 4-6 servings

Lucy's Fruit Salad and Sauces

Slice: bananas, peaches, pineapple, oranges, apples and any other fruit desired into bite-sized pieces.

Add: chopped nuts

Sauce #1

2 tablespoons honey
¼-½ cup soy, safflower, or homemade mayonnaise

Blend and pour over salad.

Sauce #2

2 tablespoons honey
¼-½ cup yogurt
½ teaspoon vanilla
dash cinnamon

Blend all ingredients and pour over fruit.

Yield: approximately ¼-½ cup

Spicy Avocado Dressing

1 ripe avocado, mashed
½ clove garlic, crushed
½ teaspoon chili powder
½ teaspoon mustard (optional)
dash lemon juice
2 tablespoons bell pepper, chopped
2 tablespoons onion, chopped
2 tablespoons celery, chopped
salt to taste

Combine all the ingredients. A good dressing or dip.

Yield: approximately 1 cup

Cottage Cheese Dressing

   4 tablespoons cottage cheese
   1 tablespoon soy mayonnaise
   1 tablespoon yogurt
   ½ teaspoon apple cider vinegar
   ½ teaspoon honey
   ¼ teaspoon marjoram
   1 teaspoon lemon juice
     dash paprika

   Blend cottage cheese, mayonnaise and yogurt
   till creamy. Add the rest of the ingredients.

Yield: ½ cup

French Dressing

   ⅓ cup tarragon or apple cider vinegar
   ¾ teaspoon honey
   ⅛ teaspoon dry mustard
   ½ teaspoon salt
   1 teaspoon garlic powder
   ⅛ teaspoon pepper
   ⅛ teaspoon cayenne pepper
   1 cup safflower oil

   Blend in blender about 35 seconds.

Yield: 1⅓ cups

Garlic Dressing

2 cloves garlic, crushed
¼ cup lemon juice
¼ cup safflower oil
    salt and cayenne pepper to taste
2 tablespoons parsley
1 teaspoon dill weed

Blend all ingredients together and let flavor develop for a few minutes before serving on salad. Try over a watercress salad garnished with hard-boiled egg slices and sunflower seeds.

           Yield: approximately ½ cup

Herbed French Dressing

⅓ cup tarragon or apple cider vinegar
¾ teaspoon honey
⅛ teaspoon dry mustard
½ teaspoon salt
1 teaspoon garlic powder
⅛ teaspoon pepper
⅛ teaspoon cayenne pepper
1 cup safflower oil
½ teaspoon marjoram
½ teaspoon thyme
½ teaspoon oregano
½ teaspoon sweet basil

Blend in blender about 35 seconds.

           Yield: 1⅓ cups

Lemon Dressing

  2 tablespoons lemon juice
  5 tablespoons safflower oil
    dash garlic powder
    dash celery seed
  ⅛ teaspoon cayenne pepper
  ½ teaspoon salt
  ½ teaspoon paprika
  ¾ teaspoon dry mustard

In a small bowl, beat lemon juice and oil well with a fork. Mix in spices. Then place in a jar and shake well before serving.

Yield: approximately ½ cup

Herbed Mayonnaise

  2 egg yolks
  ½ teaspoon salt
  1 tablespoon honey
  ½ cup tarragon vinegar
  ½ teaspoon basil
  ¼ teaspoon rosemary
    pinch cayenne pepper
  ½ teaspoon lemon juice
  ½ teaspoon dry mustard
  ½ teaspoon paprika
  1¼ cups soy or safflower oil

In blender, blend egg yolks about 5 minutes on low. Keep blending on low speed and add salt, honey and vinegar. Add basil, rosemary, cayenne, lemon juice, mustard and paprika. Add oil drop by drop to keep mayonnaise from separating.

Variation: Eliminate ½ teaspoon of lemon juice and replace ½ cup of vinegar with ½ cup of lemon juice.

Yield: 2 cups

Oil and Vinegar Dressing
(Lucy's favorite salad dressing)

6 tablespoons peanut oil
2 tablespoons wine or tarragon vinegar
¼ teaspoon dry mustard
¼ teaspoon salt
⅛ teaspoon paprika or dash cayenne pepper
   dash garlic powder

Take 1 tablespoon of the oil and 1 tablespoon of the vinegar and beat well with a fork. Add the spices and blend well. Add the remaining oil and vinegar. Beat well with a fork and serve over salad.

Yield: ½ cup dressing

Oil and Vinegar Marinade

1½ cups safflower oil
½ cup red wine vinegar or tarragon vinegar
1 teaspoon salt
¼ teaspoon peppercorns, ground
½ teaspoon dry mustard
1 teaspoon paprika
¼ teaspoon sweet basil
1 teaspoon honey
½ teaspoon garlic powder

Combine ingredients in a jar and shake well.

Yield: approximately 2 cups

Thousand Island Dressing

1 egg, medium-boiled (optional)
1 cup mayonnaise (homemade, soy or safflower)
½ cup catsup or chili sauce
  dash garlic powder
  dash lemon juice
  salt and cayenne pepper to taste

If using the egg, mash it into the mayonnaise. Add the rest of the ingredients. Stir well.

Yield: 1½ cups

Yogurt Dressing

¼ cup yogurt
½ cup lemon or orange juice
⅓ cup honey
  dash mace
  dash salt
¾ cup yogurt

In blender, blend ¼ cup yogurt, juice, honey, mace and salt. Add ¾ cup of yogurt and blend briefly.

Yield: approximately 2 cups

Yogurt-Caraway Dressing

¼ cup yogurt
3 tablespoons caraway seed
1½ teaspoons honey
  dash salt (optional)
¾ cup yogurt

Blend first 4 ingredients thoroughly, in blender. Add ¾ cup yogurt and blend briefly. Serve over salad.

Yield: 1 cup

Chapter 8

Main Events and Side Dishes

Entrees and Side Dishes

NOTES ON VEGETABLES:

1. The less vegetables are cooked, the more vitamins, minerals and enzymes they retain. So it is best to eat them raw or steamed.

2. Save juices from mild tasting vegetables for soup stock. Potato water is good to use in bread baking.

3. Leftover vegetables can be used in soups, omelets, casseroles, vegetable pie, and vegetable patties.

4. One pound of vegetables usually serves 4 to 6 people.

5. Cut vegetables diagonally to expose more of the life force.

6. There are many vitamins in the skins of vegetables, so do not remove skins from vegetables like carrots and cucumbers.

7. Yellow vegetables are rich in vitamin A.

8. Leafy green vegetables are rich in vitamins A and B.

NOTES ON POTATOES:

1. To bake: Wash and grease skins with a little oil for a tender skin. Preheat oven to 450° and bake 45 minutes. Prick with a fork after baking 15 minutes to allow air to escape and prevent exploding.

Hint: Potatoes will cook faster if placed in very hot water and completely dried before baking.

2. Potato skins are rich in minerals so always leave skin on.

NOTES ON BROWN RICE:

1. ⅓ cup uncooked rice = 1 cup cooked rice.
2. 1 cup cooked rice serves 2 people.
3. Adding Tamari soy sauce to the water in which the rice is cooked will add extra flavor.
4. Use only brown rice, as white rice has had valuable nutrients removed.

NOTES ON BEANS:

1. Soak beans overnight—3 cups of water to 1 cup of beans.

2. Add chopped onions and/or chopped garlic when soaking (especially soybeans) for extra flavor.

3. Save any water left over from soaking beans for cooking them in, adding more water as needed.

4. If you did not soak the beans the night before, cover them with water in a pot and boil 2 minutes. Remove from heat and soak an hour or 2. Then proceed to cook till tender.

5. Soybeans take longer to cook. Most beans take 45 minutes to cook. Soybeans take about 2 hours.

6. ½ cup uncooked beans yields 1 cup of cooked beans (soybeans expand a little more). One cup cooked beans serves 2.

7. Soybeans contain essential amino acids.

8. Lentils are a good source of protein.

9. Lima beans are a good source of potassium.

10. Most legumes contain vitamins B and C and phosphorus.

Stuffed Tomatoes with Broccoli

2 cups broccoli, grated
½ cup red onion, grated
1 cup sharp cheese, grated
  salt and cayenne pepper to taste
½ teaspoon basil
6-8 medium-sized tomatoes

Mix together broccoli, onion, cheese and spices. Slice stem end of tomato and scoop out pulp leaving about ¼ inch of tomato to the skin. Save pulp for a tomato sauce or other cooking uses. Fill tomato with broccoli mixture. Bake, in a shallow baking dish, 20 to 25 minutes at 325°.

Fried Cabbage

½ head cabbage
½ medium-sized onion, sliced
2 tablespoons butter
  salt and cayenne pepper to taste

Parboil cabbage and drain off water. Cut cabbage into bite-sized pieces. Saute onion in butter and add cabbage. Simmer till tender, stirring occasionally to prevent sticking. Season with salt and pepper to taste.

Yield: 4 servings

Herb Butter

    5 tablespoons butter, softened
    ¼ teaspoon parsley
    ¼ teaspoon salt
    ¼ teaspoon basil
    ½ clove garlic, crushed

Mash the ingredients into the softened butter. Spread over cauliflower right after it has been steamed and is still hot.

Variations on herb butter: add ¼ teaspoon rosemary or ¼ teaspoon thyme

Yield: approximately ¼ cup butter

Broccoli Soufflé

    2 tablespoons onion, chopped
    3 tablespoons butter
    3 tablespoons flour
    ¾ cup milk
    ½ teaspoon salt
      dash cayenne pepper
    1 cup unprocessed cheese, grated
    4 eggs, separated
    1½ pounds raw broccoli

In a large skillet, lightly sauté onion in butter. Add flour and stir to a pasty consistency. Add milk slowly and stir till smooth. Add salt, cayenne and cheese and stir till cheese is melted. Add beaten egg yolks and cool. Carefully fold in beaten egg whites. Pour over broccoli and bake 30 minutes at 350°.

Yield: 4 servings

Herbed String Beans

1 pound string beans
¼ cup butter
1 clove garlic, chopped
1 teaspoon salt
½ teaspoon sage
½ teaspoon savory

Cut the ends off the beans. Wash and steam them in a pot in a little water till they are tender, but still crunchy. In a small skillet, melt butter, and sauté garlic. Add spices, pour over beans and serve.

Yield: 4-6 servings

Brussels Sprouts and Chestnuts

1 pound chestnuts, soaked overnight in water
6 tablespoons butter
1 pound brussels sprouts
½ teaspoon salt
⅛ teaspoon white pepper
dash nutmeg
parsley for a garnish

Drain water from chestnuts and replace with fresh water. Boil 15 to 20 minutes. Peel and quarter chestnuts. In a large saucepan, melt butter, add nuts and heat till both butter and nuts are browned. In another saucepan, cook sprouts in water until tender, then drain. Add sprouts with seasonings to butter-nut sauce. Heat a few minutes and shake well to coat chestnuts and brussels sprouts with butter. Serve with parsley.

Yield: 4-6 servings

Eggs Moppioli
Preheat oven: 325°

> 6 medium-sized red potatoes
> ½ cup oil (for frying)
> 1 medium-sized onion, thinly-sliced
> 12 black Italian olives, pitted and cut into thin
>   strips
>   salt and pepper to taste
>   dash nutmeg
>   dash paprika
> ¼ cup Gruyére cheese, grated
> ¼ cup French Emmenthaler cheese, grated
> 6 eggs
> ½ cup light cream

Note: If Gruyére and Emmenthaler cheese
are not available, use ½ cup of any cheese
desired.

In a saucepan, cover unpeeled potatoes with
water and parboil them for 5 minutes.
Drain off water and cut potatoes into thin
slices. Heat oil in a large skillet. Add potatoes and onions. Brown on both sides.
Add olive strips. Cook 3 more minutes. Add
salt, pepper, nutmeg, and paprika. Place mixture in a greased, oblong baking dish. Cover
with the cheeses. Carefully break eggs, one
at a time, over the cheese. Be sure the eggs
are not touching each other. Pour the cream
over the eggs and all around the potatoes.
Bake in preheated oven for 15 minutes or
until eggs are set.

Yield: 6 servings

8 hard-boiled eggs, chopped
1 medium-sized yellow onion, finely-chopped
1 teaspoon salt
½ teaspoon pepper
½ cup *Blender Mayonnaise* (see index)
1 cucumber, peeled and thinly-sliced
  pumpernickel bread, thinly-sliced

Mix eggs, onion, salt, pepper and mayonnaise
together. Add more salt and pepper if needed.
If mixture seems dry, add more mayonnaise.
Mound the mixture on a round glass plate.
Surround with the thin slices of cucumber
and pumpernickel bread.

Yield: 6 servings

Baked Cashew Loaf
Preheat oven: 350°

2 tablespoons oil
1 cup onions, finely-chopped
1 cup celery, diced
½ cup cashews
1 cup whole wheat bread crumbs
1 teaspoon salt
½ cup milk
2 eggs, beaten

Heat oil in a skillet over moderate heat. Sauté
onions until lightly-browned. Combine in a
bowl with the rest of the ingredients. Place
in a lightly-greased loaf pan and bake in preheated oven 40 minutes.

Yield: 4 servings

Cauliflower with Herb Butter

    1 medium-sized head cauliflower
    lemon juice

Steam cauliflower and squeeze lemon juice over it. While cauliflower is steaming prepare herb butter.

Soyburgers

    2 cups soybeans, cooked
    ½ cup green pepper, chopped
    1 small onion, finely-chopped
    2 cloves garlic, finely-chopped
    ½ cup tomato puree
    2 stalks celery, chopped
    ½ teaspoon chili powder
    ½ teaspoon cumin
    ½ teaspoon dry mustard
    Tamari soy sauce, salt and cayenne pepper to taste
    *Oats, cornmeal, and wheat germ to bind

In a large bowl, mash soybeans well (or puree them). Add all the ingredients and enough grain to bind. Make 10 patties. In a skillet, fry patties on both sides in oil. Serve with lettuce and tomato.

Variation: Cheese Soyburgers—melt a slice of cheese on top after both sides have been cooked.

*Any combination of grains may be used.

Yield: 10 burgers

Vegetable Nut Roast
Preheat oven: 325°

1 cup carrots, grated
1 small onion, finely-chopped
½ cup celery, diced
¼ cup sunflower seeds
¼ cup walnuts, coarsely-chopped
1 egg, beaten
2 tablespoons butter, melted
1 tablespoon tomato juice
1 cup whole wheat bread crumbs
salt and pepper to taste

Combine all the ingredients in a bowl. Lightly grease a loaf pan and press in mixture. Bake 45 minutes in preheated oven.

Variations: 1. Replace celery with ½ cup chopped, green pepper. 2. Replace carrots with 1 cup leftover vegetables. 3. Add ½ cup chopped mushrooms.

Yield: 4 servings

Lucy's Disciple Stew

2 onions, chopped
1 green pepper, chopped
1 clove garlic, minced
12 small zucchini, sliced ¼-inch thick
1-2 fresh tomatoes, peeled
salt and cayenne pepper to taste

Sauté first 3 ingredients in a large pot. Add remaining ingredients and simmer 1 hour till stew thickens. Add a little water or tomato juice if necessary.

Yield: 6-8 servings

Cuban Black Beans

2 quarts water
1 pound black beans
1 medium-sized onion, sliced
1 green pepper, sliced
¾ cup olive oil
1 teaspoon oregano
1 bay leaf
2 tablespoons apple cider
1 teaspoon salt
¼ teaspoon pepper
1 cup brown rice, cooked (⅓ cup uncooked rice)

Combine all the ingredients except the rice in a large pot. Bring to a boil and then reduce to a low heat. Cook for 3 hours. When beans are tender, add rice and serve.

Yield: 8 servings

String Beans with Roasted Soybeans

½ red onion, sliced
2 tablespoons oil
1 cup soybeans, roasted
½ pound string beans, steamed
salt and pepper to taste

In a small skillet, sauté onion in oil till browned. After onion has absorbed most of the oil, add soybeans to warm them. Add mixture to the string beans, season with salt and pepper and serve.

Variation: Replace soybeans with cashews, raw or toasted. Yield: 4-6 servings

Pineapple-Almond Chop Suey

3 tablespoons oil
1 cup onion, chopped
1 cup celery, diced
1 cup white cabbage, shredded
3 tablespoons vegetable water or stock
1 cup bean sprouts
1 cup pineapple chunks
2 tablespoons Tamari soy sauce
1 cup almonds, slivered
3 cups brown rice, cooked (1 cup uncooked rice)

Heat oil in a large, moderately-hot skillet.
Add onions, celery and cabbage. Stir and fry
about 3 minutes. Add vegetable water or
stock. Cover with a lid and steam about 5
minutes. Then add bean sprouts, pineapple,
soy sauce and almonds. Steam till sprouts and
pineapple are hot. Serve immediately over
rice.

Yield: 6 servings

Lucy's Vegetarian Style Chili

1 pound pinto beans, soaked overnight and
cooked till tender
6 whole tomatoes, peeled
1 onion, chopped
1 clove garlic, chopped
salt and cayenne pepper to taste
3 tablespoons chili powder
1 teaspoon cumin seed

In a large pot, mix all ingredients and simmer
a few hours until mixture is very thick.
Excellent with corn bread.

Yield: 4-6 servings

Soybean-Lentil-Rice Loaf
Preheat oven: 350°

    1 cup cooked soybeans
    1 cup cooked lentils
    1 cup cooked brown rice
    ¾ cup milk, water, stock or gravy
    1 medium-sized onion, finely-chopped
    2 cloves garlic, finely-chopped
    1 egg, beaten
    ¼ cup tomato puree
    2 stalks celery, chopped
    2 teaspoons salt
    cayenne pepper to taste

In a large mixing bowl, mash soybeans and lentils well. Add the rest of the ingredients and mix. Turn into an oiled loaf pan. Bake in preheated oven for 1 hour. Serve as is or with *Tomato Sauce* (see index). This is a meat loaf substitute.

Yield: 6 servings

Lentil Sheperd's Pie
Preheat oven: 400°

    2 cups cooked lentils
    1 small onion, chopped
    1 teaspoon sage
    dash oregano
    1 teaspoon salt
    dash cayenne pepper
    1 large cooked potato
    small amount hot milk
    butter
    salt

In a large mixing bowl, mash cooked lentils. Add onions and seasonings. Put in a lightly-oiled casserole dish. In a separate bowl, mash potato and add hot milk, with butter and salt. Beat till fluffy. Spread on top of lentils and bake for 20 minutes in preheated oven. Put under broiler to brown the top and serve.

Yield: 4 servings

Lentil Roast
Preheat oven: 350°

2 cups lentils, cooked and pureed
1 cup tomato puree
1 small onion, chopped
few stalks celery, chopped
1 cup whole wheat bread crumbs
1 teaspoon salt
¼ teaspoon cayenne pepper
1 clove garlic, chopped
1 green pepper, sliced in rings

In a large mixing bowl, combine all the ingredients except the green pepper rings. Turn into an oiled loaf pan and top with the green pepper rings. Bake 40 minutes, covered, in preheated oven.

Hint: Sprinkle wheat germ on top for added vitamin E.

Yield: 4-6 servings

Grainburgers

⅔ cup rice, uncooked
2 cups water
1 teaspoon salt
⅓ cup green pepper, chopped
⅓ cup onion, chopped
⅓ cup celery, chopped
1 egg (optional)
⅓ cup cornmeal
⅓ cup oats
⅓ cup wheat germ
　 soy flour or other flour
　 Tamari soy sauce to taste
　 salt and cayenne pepper to taste

Rice should be sticky when cooked. Cook rice in a pot with water and salt. Cool and add the vegetables. Stir in the egg if desired. Add grains and enough soy flour to hold mixture together. Season to taste. Make into 9 patties. If patty seems too sticky, dip in flour. Brown in oil, on both sides, in hot skillet. Serve with lettuce and tomatoes.

Cheese Grainburgers: Add a slice of cheese, when both sides are browned, and continue cooking until cheese has melted.

Note: This mixture will keep for several days covered, in the refrigerator.

Yield: 9 burgers

Baked Carrots and Apples
Preheat oven: 350°

1 cup carrots, shredded
2 medium-sized apples, grated
½ cup coconut, shredded
⅓ cup honey
3 tablespoons butter, melted
    dash salt
1 teaspoon cinnamon
1 teaspoon lemon juice

In a large mixing bowl, mix all ingredients and put into a lightly-oiled casserole dish. Bake 25 minutes in preheated oven.

Yield: 4 servings

Glazed Carrots and Raisins

½-1 cup raisins
6 medium-sized carrots, sliced diagonally and thin
2 tablespoons butter
3 tablespoons maple syrup or 2½ tablespoons honey and ½ teaspoon molasses
½ teaspoon orange rind, grated
    dash ginger powder or a little grated ginger root

In a pot, cover raisins with water and boil a few minutes. Drain water into another pot and set raisins aside. Steam carrots in raisin water, adding more water if necessary. Melt butter in a skillet with maple syrup, orange rind, and ginger. Add raisins and carrots and coat well.

Variation: Omit orange rind and ginger. Add ½ teaspoon mint leaves.

Yield: 6 servings

Lucy's Eggplant Casserole
Preheat oven: 350°

1 eggplant, cut into small chunks
2-3 cups stewed tomatoes
6 mushrooms, sliced
1 onion, chopped
salt and cayenne pepper to taste
1 cup Romano cheese, grated

In a saucepan, simmer eggplant and tomatoes over low heat till eggplant is soft and clear looking, about 15 minutes. Meanwhile, sauté mushrooms and onion in a small skillet. Pour into greased casserole dish: the eggplant and tomatoes, mushrooms, and onion, seasoned with salt and pepper. Top with grated cheese and bake in a preheated oven for 20 minutes.

Yield: 4 servings

Fried Eggplant

1 medium-sized eggplant
2 eggs, beaten
1-2 cups cracker or bread crumbs
oil for frying
salt to taste

Slice eggplant about ¼-inch thick with or without skin. Dip both sides in egg and then in cracker crumbs, coating slices well. Fry in hot oil in skillet. Brown on both sides. Oil should be ¼ to ½-inch deep. Salt to taste. The secret of good fried eggplant is to cook it slowly.

Variation: Replace eggplant with sliced zucchini or cucumbers or use in combination.

Yield: 4 servings

For Eggplant Lovers
Preheat oven: 300°

1 medium-sized eggplant
  butter
½ onion, sliced in rings
  mushrooms, sliced thin
  Romano cheese, grated
  salt to taste

Wash and slice eggplant ¼-inch thick. Lightly butter both sides and bake in a casserole dish, in a preheated oven till eggplant is tender, about 12 minutes. Meanwhile, in a small skillet, lightly saute onion rings and mushrooms and grated cheese. Salt to taste. Pop under broiler for a few minutes. Serve as is, or with a *Tomato Sauce* (see index).   Yield: 3-4 servings

Lucy's Eggplant Steaks

⅔ cup milk
2 eggs, beaten
1 cup whole wheat flour
1 medium-sized eggplant, sliced
  oil for frying

In a medium-sized mixing bowl, add milk to eggs and blend. Sift in flour and stir until mixture is well blended. Batter should be thick so add more flour if necessary. Dip eggplant in batter and slowly saute in ¼ to ½-inch of oil in cast iron skillet, till eggplant can be easily pierced with a fork.

Yield: 4 servings

141

Eggplant Parmigiana
Preheat oven: 350°

> ¼ cup butter
> 1 egg, beaten
> ¼ teaspoon salt
> ¼ teaspoon pepper
> 6 slices eggplant, ½-inch thick
> 1 cup whole wheat bread crumbs
> 3 cups *Tomato Sauce* (see index)
> 6 slices mozzarella cheese
> 2 tablespoons Parmesan cheese

Heat butter in a moderately hot skillet. Beat egg with salt and pepper. Dip eggplant slices in egg and then in the bread crumbs, completely coating the slice. Sauté both sides until browned. Lay in a shallow baking dish. Pour tomato sauce over the eggplant. Then cover with mozzarella cheese. Sprinkle Parmesan cheese over the mozzarella cheese. Bake in a preheated oven for 30 minutes or until cheese is melted and lightly-browned.

Yield: 4 servings

Stuffed Butternut Squash Halves
Preheat oven: 350°

> 2 butternut squash
> 4 tablespoons butter
> 2 tablespoons oil
> 1 cup mushrooms, chopped
> 1 cup onions, chopped
> 4 tablespoons plain yogurt
> 1 cup carrots, grated
> ¼ cup wheat germ

Cut squash in half lengthwise. Remove seeds. Place 1 tablespoon of butter in each squash cavity. Bake in a shallow baking dish until tender, about 45 minutes in a pre-heated oven. While the squash is baking, heat oil in a skillet. Add the mushrooms and onions and sauté until lightly-browned. Set aside. Remove squash from oven and carefully scoop the cooked squash from the shells. Mash with yogurt and combine with the sautéed mushrooms and onions, carrots, and wheat germ. Refill squash halves and return to oven for 10 minutes.

Yield: 4 servings

Steamed Zucchini and Tomatoes

2 green onions, sliced with stems
1 tablespoon oil
2 medium-sized zucchini, sliced
2 medium-sized tomatoes, thinly-wedged
  bay leaf
  garlic powder or 1 clove garlic, minced
  Tamari soy sauce
  salt and pepper to taste

Sauté green onions in a large skillet in the oil. Add the sliced zucchini and sauté 5 minutes. Add the tomatoes and bay leaf with a little water. Steam, covered, until tomatoes are tender. Add garlic, a few dashes of soy sauce, salt and pepper to taste. Remove bay leaf and serve.

Yield: 4 servings

143

Ratatouille (Ra-ta-too-ee)

- 1 eggplant, cut in cubes
- 2 tablespoons oil (olive is nice)
- 2 tablespoons butter
- 1 onion, chopped
- 2 green peppers, seeded and chopped
- 4 zucchini squash, cut in cubes
- 4-6 tomatoes, cut in cubes
- 2 cloves garlic, chopped
- 2 tablespoons parsley, chopped
- 1 teaspoon oregano
- ½ cup Parmesan cheese, grated
  salt and pepper to taste

In a large skillet, sauté eggplant in oil and butter carefully till tender. Remove eggplant from pan. Add more oil and butter to the skillet if necessary and sauté the onions, peppers, zucchini and tomatoes. Combine all the ingredients. Place in oiled baking dish and bake at 300° for 15 minutes.

Yield: 8 servings

Baked Butternut Squash
Preheat oven: 350°

- 1 medium-sized butternut squash
- 1 tablespoon butter
- 2 tablespoons honey
- 1 tablespoon molasses
- 2 tablespoons orange juice
- 1 teaspoon cinnamon
  dash ginger
  orange peel, grated (optional)

Peel skin off squash and cut squash into slices ½-inch thick. Lay slices in a baking dish. In a small saucepan, heat, on low, butter, honey, molasses and juice, just enough to get them mixed well. Pour over squash and sprinkle the top with cinnamon, ginger and orange peel. Bake in a preheated oven for 45 minutes, basting occasionally with orange juice mixture.

Yield: 3-4 servings

Variations: 1. Sprinkle wheat germ or nuts over casserole before serving. 2. Add ½ cup raisins the last 5 minutes of baking.

Stuffed Zucchini Boats
Preheat oven: 350°

Allow 1 medium-sized squash per person if serving as a main dish

1 cup apple, finely-chopped
½ cup celery, finely-chopped
¼ cup raisins
¼ cup almonds, chopped
1 green onion, finely-chopped

Wash zucchini and cook it about 2 minutes, in salted water. Drain and let squash cool. Slice in half lengthwise. Scoop out center of squash leaving about ¼-inch on the skin. In a mixing bowl, combine remaining ingredients. Fill the squash with the mixture and bake for 20 minutes in a preheated oven. Place side by side in an oblong baking pan or use a cookie sheet. Eat as is, or serve with *Basic Cream Sauce* (see index).

Lucy's Zucchini-Custard Casserole
Preheat oven: 350°

2 pounds zucchini (about 4 cups), sliced
1 tablespoon onion, minced
¼ cup butter, melted
3 eggs
½ cup milk or cream
⅓ cup Parmesan or other cheese, grated
2 tablespoons dry bread crumbs (optional)
¾ teaspoon salt
   dash cayenne pepper
½ cup Parmesan cheese, grated

In a large skillet, saute zucchini and onion in butter till tender. Set aside. In a large mixing bowl, beat eggs and milk. Add ⅓ cup of cheese, bread crumbs, salt and pepper to milk and eggs. Stir in zucchini and onion. Turn mixture into buttered, 1½-quart casserole dish. Sprinkle top with ½ cup of grated cheese. Bake, uncovered, in a preheated oven for 35 to 40 minutes.

Yield: as a main course 2-3 servings
      as a side dish 4-6 servings

Herbed Peas

2 cups peas, steamed
½ teaspoon basil
½ teaspoon salt
1 teaspoon parsley flakes
¼ teaspoon rosemary

Add seasonings to peas or try the steamed peas with chopped onion. Add salt to taste and a squeeze of lemon juice.

Yield: 4 servings

Divine Mushroom Casserole
Preheat oven: 300°

1 onion, chopped
2 cloves garlic, chopped
1 pound mushrooms, chopped
2 tablespoons parsley, chopped
4 tablespoons butter
4 tablespoons oil
1 cup bread crumbs
⅓ cup sherry or white wine
¼ cup broth or stock
½ teaspoon marjoram
  salt and cayenne pepper to taste
½ teaspoon rosemary
  dash of kelp (optional)
  dash of brewer's yeast (optional)
2 eggs
4 cups cooked grains (rice, wheat berries, barley, etc.)
½ cup sharp cheese, grated

In a large skillet, saute onion, garlic, mushrooms and parsley in butter and oil till onions are almost golden brown. Add crumbs, sherry, broth and seasonings. Cook a minute more. Beat eggs in a bowl, add grains and mix well. Add contents of skillet to grain and egg mixture and mix well. Turn into oiled casserole dish and top with cheese. Bake in preheated oven for 30 minutes.

Yield: 4-6 servings

147

Mushroom Burgers

2 cups mushrooms, raw and chopped
1 tablespoon butter
dash nutmeg
salt and cayenne pepper to taste
1 egg, beaten
¼ cup onion, chopped
¼ cup green pepper, chopped
1 cup whole wheat bread crumbs

In a small skillet, sauté mushrooms in butter. Season with nutmeg, salt and cayenne. Place mushrooms in a mixing bowl with the beaten egg. Add onion, green pepper and crumbs and shape into patties. Add more bread crumbs if needed to hold together. Fry patties in a little butter in a hot skillet. Melt a slice of cheese on top for cheese-mushroom burgers. Serve with lettuce and tomatoes.

Yield: 4-5 servings

Succotash

½ cup peas
½ cup lima beans
½ cup water
½ cup corn
½ cup zucchini, chopped
½ cup red pepper (bell), chopped
½ cup onion, chopped
1 clove garlic, chopped
butter or oil for sautéing
basil to taste
rosemary to taste
salt and pepper to taste

In a large saucepan, cook peas and lima beans in water, about 2 to 3 minutes, over medium heat. Add corn, cut off the cob. After 2 minutes add zucchini (lower heat), add red pepper. In a small skillet, sauté onion and garlic in butter or oil. Add to vegetables when all the water has been used up. Season to taste.

Yield: 3 servings

Spinach-Mushroom Rolls

1 pound fresh spinach
   squeeze lemon juice
   salt to taste
¼ pound fresh mushrooms, sliced
2 green onions, chopped with stems
   oil for sautéing
6-8 Chappati (see index) with ¼ cup chopped
     onion added to flour

Wash spinach well. In a covered saucepan, steam spinach until tender in a small amount of water. Season with lemon juice and salt. In a large skillet, sauté mushrooms and onions in oil and add them to spinach. In the same skillet, roll out chappati and fry them in oil. Don't fry them crisp, be sure they are flexible enough to roll. Fill chappati with spinach mixture. Stick a toothpick in the center to hold closed. Lay side by side in a baking dish and bake 15 minutes at 325°. Eat as they are, or serve with *Gravy* or *Basic Cheese Sauce* (see index).

Yield: 6-8 rolls

Easley Farm Vegetable Pies
Preheat oven: 350°

> 2 tablespoons oil
> ¾ cup cauliflower, grated
> ¾ cup carrots, grated
> ¾ cup zucchini squash, grated
> ¾ cup onion, grated
>   salt and pepper to taste
> 9 *Chappati* (see index)

> Heat oil in a large skillet. Add the grated raw vegetables. Cook until tender but still crisp. Season to taste with salt and pepper. Roll chappati and fill each one with ⅓ cup of the filling. Fold the chappati and seal the edges together by pinching them with your fingers. Do this for all 9 pies. Bake in a shallow baking dish, in a preheated oven, till browned.

> Yield: 9 pies

Vegetable Curry

> 2 tablespoons butter
> 3 cups cooked brown rice (1 cup uncooked rice)
> ⅓ cup zucchini, thinly-sliced
> ½ cup yellow squash, thinly-sliced
> ¼ cup green pepper, chopped
> 1 small tomato, sliced in thin strips
> 1 teaspoon celery salt
>   dash pepper
> 1 tablespoon curry powder
> 2 tablespoons water

> Heat butter in a large skillet with a cover.

Add the rice and brown on all sides over a moderate heat. Add the vegetables, seasonings and water. Cover skillet with a lid. Turn heat to low. Simmer until vegetables are tender.

Yield: 6 servings

Summer Squash Casserole

2 eggs, beaten
½ cup wheat germ
1 teaspoon salt
  dash cayenne pepper
1 teaspoon Tamari soy sauce
3 cups summer squash (yellow squash) unpeeled and pureed in a blender
¼ pound mushrooms, sliced
½ onion, sliced in rings
1 green pepper, sliced in rings
  paprika to top

In a large mixing bowl, add eggs, wheat germ and seasonings to pureed squash. Pour ½ of the puree into an oiled casserole dish. Then put a layer of ½ of the mushrooms, a layer of ½ of the onion rings, and a layer of ½ of the green pepper rings. Pour the other half of the puree into the baking dish. Top with the remaining mushrooms, green pepper and onion rings and sprinkle with paprika. Bake at 350° till browned on top.

Variations: Add a few slices of cheese and melt under broiler before serving.

Yield: 4 servings

Vegetarian Homemade Pizza

    1 tablespoon honey
    1 cup lukewarm water
    1 tablespoon yeast
    1 teaspoon salt
    2 tablespoons oil
    4 cups whole wheat flour
    3 cups *Tomato Sauce* (see index)
    ¼ cup mushrooms, chopped
    1 pepper, seeded and cut in rings
    1 carrot, grated
    ½ cup, unprocessed cheese, grated (optional)

Dissolve honey in water. Sprinkle in yeast and let stand 5 minutes. Add salt, oil and flour and knead about 10 minutes on a floured board. Let rise 2 hours. Reknead and let rise another 30 minutes. Roll out dough with a rolling pin and pinch edges to make a thick crust to hold the sauce. Bake dough 30 minutes at 400°. Spread sauce over dough and add mushrooms, green pepper rings, carrots or whatever vegetables you like. Bake 15 more minutes with sauce at 350°. Add cheese if desired and pop under broiler a minute to melt it.   Yield: 2 large pizzas

Stuffed Potatoes

Bake potatoes and remove from oven. Cool a little and cut potatoes in half. Scoop out insides and mash them with hot milk and butter. Beat till fluffy and salt to taste. Return to skin jackets, top with grated unprocessed cheese and paprika. Return to oven and reheat to melt cheese.

152

Mashed Potatoes

In a saucepan, boil potatoes with skins till tender. Peel and mash with a potato masher or fork. Add hot milk and butter and beat till fluffy. Season with salt and a dash of cayenne pepper.

Variation: Try adding a little garlic powder or sauteed onion for extra flavor.

Vegetable Stew

2 cups potatoes, cubed
1 small onion, cut into rings
1 cup carrots, sliced
½ cup celery, chopped
1 cup peas
1 cup string beans
3 tomatoes, wedged
2 bay leaves
  salt and pepper to taste
1 teaspoon basil

In a saucepan, boil potatoes about 10 minutes. Drain potatoes, saving water. In a big pot, lightly saute potatoes and all the vegetables except the tomatoes. Add 1 to 2 cups of water (including the leftover potato water). Add bay leaves and simmer till vegetables are almost tender, then add tomatoes, salt, pepper, and basil. Warm and serve. A good, filling meal when served with homemade bread.

Yield: 6 servings

Potato Ring

8 large potatoes
¼ pound butter
2 tablespoons onion, chopped
2 tablespoons parsley, chopped
½ teaspoon garlic powder
¼ cup black olives, sliced (optional)
salt and pepper to taste
caraway seeds

In a large saucepan, parboil potatoes. When cool, peel and chop. Add butter, onion, parsley, garlic, olives, salt and pepper to taste. Add more garlic and onions if desired. Mix thoroughly and pour into large, well-greased ring mold and sprinkle with caraway seeds. Bake in 400° oven till brown. This also may be browned in a skillet and served as a potato pancake.

Yield: 8 servings

Hashed Brown Potatoes

Grate or dice, raw or cooked potatoes. Cook in a hot, oiled skillet till both sides are browned. Add grated onion for extra flavor. Raw potatoes will take about 35 minutes to brown, and cooked potatoes will take about 20 minutes to brown. Season with salt and a dash of cayenne pepper.

Hint: One secret of good hash browns is lots of paprika on both sides. This will make them really brown. Sprinkle it on potatoes as they begin to cook in the frying pan.

Aunt Betty's Peapods

1 onion, chopped
1 tablespoon oil
½ cup water
1 teaspoon salt
½ pound mushrooms, sliced
1 pound peapods
  butter

Sauté onion in oil in heavy dutch oven or frying pan. When browned add water, salt, mushrooms and peapods. Cover and let steam until crunchy, about 5 minutes or so. Dot with butter and serve.   Yield: 4-6 servings

Noodles and Broccoli

1 bunch broccoli
2 quarts water
1 teaspoon salt
1 pound whole wheat noodles
1 pint mushrooms, sliced
1 stick butter
1 cup Parmesan cheese, grated
  salt and pepper to taste
1 fresh tomato, chopped

Chop the broccoli into medium-sized pieces. In a large pot, boil broccoli in water with salt for about 5 minutes. Add noodles and continue cooking for about 10 minutes (or until noodles are tender). Drain and set aside. Meanwhile, in a small skillet, sauté mushrooms in butter. Add mushrooms to broccoli and noodles. Add cheese, salt and pepper and tomato. Toss lightly. Serve immediately.

Yield: 6 servings

155

Good Friday Noodles

    1 pound whole wheat noodles
    1 tablespoon oil
    ¼ cup butter
    1½ cups yogurt
    2 tablespoons soy powder or flour
    1 tablespoon poppy seeds
    1 cup raisins or pitted prunes
    3 tablespoons honey
    1 cup croutons (or toasted bread cubes)

Cook noodles in large pot of boiling water with oil. Stir often and cook till tender. Drain. Put noodles back in pot over low heat and mix in remaining ingredients. Heat thoroughly and serve.

Variations: Add ¼ cup coconut milk and ¼ cup grated coconut.

Yield: 4 servings

Noodle Kugel

    10 ounces medium-wide, whole wheat noodles
    1 tablespoon oil
    4 eggs, beaten
    ⅓ cup butter, melted
    1 apple, chopped
    ½ cup nuts, chopped
    ⅔ cup raisins
    ⅓ cup honey
    ½ teaspoon salt
    2 tablespoons strawberry preserves
    1 lemon, grated with rind
    1 teaspoon cinnamon

In a large pot, boil noodles in water with oil,
until tender. Drain and wash with cold
water. Combine with the rest of the ingredients and turn into lightly oiled, oblong
baking dish. Bake at 325° for 1 hour. To serve,
cut into squares.

Yield: 4-6 servings

Lucy's Macaroni and Cheese a la Pizza

2 tablespoons butter
2 tablespoons whole wheat flour
1 cup milk
1 cup grated cheese
8 ounces wheat-soy macaroni, cooked and
    drained
3 fresh tomatoes, chopped
½ teaspoon or more basil
½ teaspoon oregano
    salt and cayenne pepper to taste
    cheese slices for top

In a large saucepan, melt butter and remove
from heat. Add flour and stir to make a paste.
Add milk, gradually, and stir till thick. Add
grated cheese. Mix macaroni and tomatoes
into cheese sauce. Bake, topped with basil,
oregano, salt and pepper and sliced cheese,
in an uncovered casserole dish at 400° for
20 minutes.

Yield: 4 servings

157

Macaroni and Cheese Casserole

8 ounces wheat-soy macaroni
1 tablespoon oil
6-8 ounces milk yellow cheese, cut into chunks
½ cup milk
  salt and cayenne pepper to taste

In a large pot, boil macaroni in water with oil, until tender. Drain in a colander and rinse with cold water. Place in casserole dish. Mix in cheese chunks. Add milk, salt and pepper to taste. Bake uncovered 45 minutes at 350°.   Yield: 4-6 servings

Deluxe Macaroni Casserole

8 ounces wheat-soy macaroni
1 tablespoon oil
¼ pound mushrooms, sliced
½ cup celery, chopped
1 small onion, chopped
2 tablespoons oil for sautéing
1 cup bean sprouts
1 cup *Basic Cheese Sauce* (see index)
  salt and cayenne pepper to taste
1 tomato, wedged

In a large pot, boil macaroni in water with 1 tablespoon of oil, until tender. Drain in a colander and rinse with cold water. In a small skillet, sauté mushrooms, celery and onion in 2 tablespoons of oil. Add to macaroni along with sprouts, cheese sauce and salt and pepper. Bake, uncovered, in a casserole dish for 45 minutes at 350°. Add tomato on top and serve.   Yield: 4-6 servings

158

Garlic Cheesegrits
Preheat oven: 350°

1 cup soy grits
4 cups water
½ teaspoon salt
¼ pound butter
1 heaping teaspoon garlic powder
½ pound sharp cheese, grated
1 teaspoon Tamari soy sauce
  paprika

In a medium-sized saucepan, cook grits in salted water until they have absorbed the water and are tender. Add butter, garlic powder, grated cheese and Tamari soy sauce. Stir until butter is melted. Put grits in a greased casserole. Sprinkle paprika over the top. Bake in preheated oven 15 to 20 minutes.

Yield: 4 servings

Simple Browned Rice

2 tablespoons oil (peanut is nice)
2 cups cooked rice
1 teaspoon paprika
  salt and cayenne pepper to taste
  Tamari soy sauce to taste

Heat oil in skillet and add rice. Sprinkle with paprika. Brown 10 to 20 minutes. Season with salt, pepper and soy sauce. A good way to use leftover rice.

Yield: 4 servings

Spaghetti Dinner

    12 ounces buckwheat or soy spaghetti
    1 tablespoon oil
    In a large pot, cook spaghetti in water with
    oil until spaghetti is tender. Drain and rinse
    with cold water.

Sauce:

    4 tablespoons olive oil
    ½ onion, chopped
    ½ green pepper, chopped
    3 stalks celery, chopped
    ¼ pound mushrooms, sliced
    1 clove garlic, chopped
    1 quart tomato puree
    1 teaspoon honey
    1 bay leaf
    salt, cayenne pepper, basil and oregano to
        taste

In a heavy saucepan, mix first 6 ingredients.
Add remaining ingredients and simmer sauce
45 minutes. Serve over spaghetti. Refrigerate
leftover sauce.

Yield: 6 servings

Variations on sauce: Add diced eggplant, or
3 bay leaves.

Note: If sauce is too thick, add a little water
to thin out, or replace part of the tomato
puree with tomato juice.

Rice Stuffed Cabbage Leaves

12 cabbage leaves
12 fresh mushrooms, sliced
2 cups cooked rice
¼ cup celery, chopped
½ onion, sliced
1 tablespoon parsley, chopped
1 teaspoon sage
  garlic powder to taste
  Tamari soy sauce to taste
1 cup cheese, grated (optional)

In a large pot, parboil head of cabbage till leaves may be carefully removed, one at a time. They should be somewhat flexible. In a small skillet, sauté mushrooms. Put rice in large mixing bowl and add mushrooms. Add celery, onion, parsley, sage and garlic powder to taste. Season with soy sauce. Fill lower end of each leaf with stuffing and sprinkle grated cheese over the top of the rice mixture. Roll leaf once. Fold sides of leaf toward the center. Continue rolling to the end. Tie with string or secure with a toothpick to prevent cabbage from unrolling. Lay leaves side by side in a baking dish. Bake 20 minutes at 350°.

Yield: 6 servings

Baked Rice with Cheese Sauce
Preheat oven: 325°

2 cups rice, cooked
1 cup *Basic Cheese Sauce* (see index) with ¼
    teaspoon dry mustard
2 tablespoons parsley, chopped
2 tablespoons caraway seeds for topping

Oil a casserole dish and pour rice and cheese
sauce in it. Top with chopped parsley and
caraway seeds. Bake in preheated oven for
30 minutes. For a browned top, pop under
the broiler for a minute before serving.

Yield: 4 servings

Lucy's Mexican Fried Rice

3-4 cups cooked brown rice
1-2 cups fresh corn
2-3 fresh tomatoes, cubed
2 scallions, diced
    butter, peanut or salad oil for sautéing
¼ teaspoon paprika
    salt, cayenne pepper and Tamari soy sauce

In 2 cast iron skillets, sauté first 4 ingredients
in oil or butter till rice and vegetables are
browned. Add seasonings and serve.

Variations: 1. Add chopped green and red
(not the hot kind) pepper. 2. Add 1 clove of
chopped garlic. 3. Add ½ to 1 teaspoon of
chili powder.

Yield: 6 servings

Rice Chop Suey

3 cups rice, cooked
½ cup celery, chopped
½ cup green pepper, sliced
¾ cup onion, sliced in rings
10 water chestnuts, sliced
½ cup bamboo shoots (optional)
½ pound mushrooms
2 tablespoons oil
  Lightly sauté rice and vegetables in the oil in a heavy frying pan.

Gravy:

2 tablespoons butter
1 tablespoon onion, chopped
2 tablespoons whole wheat flour
1 cup vegetable stock
¼ teaspoon honey
¼ teaspoon salt
½ teaspoon Tamari soy sauce

  Make gravy by melting butter in a small skillet, browning onion in it, and stirring in flour to make a paste. Slowly add stock, honey, salt and soy sauce. Simmer a few minutes. Add to the vegetables and simmer 10 to 15 minutes. When done, serve over the rice and vegetables.

Variation: Top with bean spouts.

Yield: 5-6 servings

Rice Stuffed Zucchini

4 zucchini squash
2 cups cooked rice
1 tablespoon parsley, finely-chopped
2 medium-sized tomatoes, chopped
1 clove garlic, chopped
1 medium-sized onion, chopped
  salt to taste
  dash cayenne pepper
½ teaspoon oregano
⅛ teaspoon sage

Wash whole zucchini, cut off one end and remove core with serrated grapefruit knife. Leave ½ inch at the other end so filling will not fall out. Repeat for each squash. In a mixing bowl, mix the rest of the ingredients to make rice stuffing. Fill each zucchini with rice stuffing. Wrap each zucchini in aluminum foil and stand all of them upright in soup pot. Add about 2 inches of water, cover, and bring to a boil. Turn heat to low and allow to steam for 1 hour, adding water when necessary.

Yield: 4 servings

Variation: After steaming zucchini may be sliced and sautéed in butter.

Note: If you are only cooking for about 4 to 6 people—when placing zucchini in soup pot, place uncut end of the zucchini against the bottom outer rim of the pot and let them fall toward the center so that the tips meet and balance each other upright.

Gnocchi
(Rice or Potato Substitute)

2 cups milk
½ cup yellow cornmeal
1½ teaspoons honey
1 teaspoon salt
1 cup Parmesan or Swiss cheese, grated
4 tablespoons butter, soft
2 eggs, beaten

Scald milk over double boiler. Gradually add cornmeal. Then add honey and salt. Cover and let stand on low heat for 20 minutes. Remove from heat. Add ½ cup of the cheese and 2 tablespoons of the butter. Add eggs. Spread ½-inch thick in a greased, shallow casserole dish. Cool, and chill overnight if possible. Before baking, spread remaining ½ cup of cheese and 2 tablespoons of butter over top of casserole. Bake 30 minutes in a 375° oven.

Yield: 6 servings

Rice Stuffed Peppers

4 bell peppers
1 small onion, chopped
  few stalks celery, chopped
10 mushrooms, sliced
2 tablespoons oil
2 cups cooked rice
  Tomato Sauce (see index)
1 cup cheese, grated

Wash peppers, remove stem end and inside seeds. In a large pot, parboil peppers, remove from pot and allow peppers to dry. In a large skillet, sauté onion, celery and mushrooms in oil. Add rice, tomato sauce and cheese to skillet and simmer a few minutes. Fill peppers with rice stuffing and place them on a cookie sheet. Place in oven and bake for about 20 minutes at 350°. A good meal with corn on the cob and salad.

Yield: 4 servings

Baked Rice-Raisin-Nut Casserole
Preheat oven: 350°

½ cup mushrooms, sliced
1 tablespoon oil
  dash nutmeg
2 cups rice, cooked
½ cup raisins
¼ cup almonds, chopped
¼ cup sunflower seeds
  salt and cayenne pepper to taste
  sesame seeds to sprinkle on top

In a small skillet, sauté the mushrooms in the oil and season with a dash of nutmeg. In a mixing bowl, combine all ingredients except sesame seeds. Place in an oiled casserole dish, sprinkle sesame seeds on top and bake 30 minutes in preheated oven.

Variation: Use ½ cup wild rice (eliminate sunflower seeds). Add ½ cup sliced water chestnuts, ½ cup celery, and 1 small onion, sliced.
In a small skillet, sauté chestnuts, celery and onion with mushrooms. Add more oil as needed. Season with Tamari soy sauce.

Yield: 4-6 servings

Date Yam Supreme
Preheat oven: 350°

2 cups yams, cooked till tender
  a little milk and a little butter
1 cup pecans, chopped
1 cup bananas, mashed
1 cup dates, chopped
½ cup honey
1 tablespoon orange juice
¼ teaspoon salt

Mash yams with milk and butter. Beat till fluffy. Add the rest of the ingredients, blending well. Pour into greased casserole dish. Bake 20 to 25 minutes in preheated oven. Place under broiler to brown the top.

Yield: 4-6 servings

Fried Yams and Vegetables

1 turnip, parboiled and sliced
2 medium-sized yams, parboiled and sliced
1 large parsnip, sliced paper-thin
1 carrot, thinly-sliced
½ onion, sliced in rings
10 mushrooms, sliced
2 tablespoons maple syrup or honey in each skillet
1 tablespoon molasses in each skillet

Mix turnip, yams, parsnip, carrot and onion in a large bowl. Heat 2 well-oiled skillets. Divide the vegetables in half and fry in 2 skillets. When nearly browned, add ½ the mushrooms, honey and molasses to each skillet. Add more oil as needed. Be sure the honey and molasses coat the vegetables well.

Yield: 4-6 servings

Chapter 9

Sweet Things

Notes on Cookies:

1. Remove cookies from cookie sheet immediately.

2. Cookie batter will keep refrigerated a few days so bake just what is needed at the time, and bake the rest a few days later.

3. Put a slice of bread in with cookies when you store them. This will keep them moist and fresh longer.

Notes on Baking Cakes:

1. When pouring cake batter, pour first into corners and sides of pan.

2. Test for finished cake:
   a. Cake has pulled away from sides.
   b. A toothpick stuck in the center is removed dry.
   c. The top springs back when lightly touched.

3. A good way to mix the liquid ingredients of a cake is in the blender.

4. Test for stiffly-beaten egg whites: When the bowl is tipped the egg whites don't slide.

5. To crack a coconut, first puncture the eyes with a screwdriver and let the juice drain into a cup. (Drink juice or save for cooking uses.) Crack coconut with a hammer and remove the shell, or place in a hot oven, about 400°, for about 20 minutes, then crack with ham-

mer and remove shell. To toast coconut, shred it and spread out in a shallow pan and broil it a few minutes, till lightly-browned. This yields 3 to 4 cups of shredded coconut for one medium-sized coconut.

6. Heat raisins and dried fruit before adding them to batter. This prevents them from sinking to the bottom.

7. One medium-sized lemon yields 3 tablespoons of lemon juice and 1 tablespoon grated rind.

8. Line a cake pan with greased waxed paper for easy removal of cake.

9. ⅞ cup whole wheat flour is equivalent to 1 cup of white flour.

10. I find heating the cake pan before adding the batter helps the cake rise.

Notes on Pie Crust:

1. Chill pie dough to make rolling it easier.

2. A good way to roll dough is between 2 pieces of waxed paper.

3. Handle pie dough as little as possible.

4. Whole wheat pastry flour, or unbleached white flour with wheat germ added makes the lightest crust.

5. Try substituting orange, apple or pineapple juice for water in a pie crust recipe.

6. Add grated lemon or orange rind to dough for flavor.

7. For added crunch and texture, put ground nuts or seeds in dough.

Cooking with Honey:

1. Replace 1 cup of sugar with ¾ cup of honey. Reduce liquid in recipe by ¼.

Example: Recipe calls for 1 cup sugar and ½ cup oil, use ¾ cup honey and ⅜ cup oil

170

2. Lightly oil measuring cup before measuring honey, molasses, or maple syrup and the sweeteners will pour out with ease.

Carob vs. Chocolate

Carob, also called St. John's Bread, comes from carob pods that grow on trees. It tastes similar to chocolate, yet contains no chocolate or cocoa to which many people are allergic.

Carob contains only one-hundredth the amount of fat found in chocolate and carob is much richer in calcium.

Carob Brownies
Preheat oven: 350°

1 stick butter, softened
1 cup raw sugar
½ tablespoon vanilla
2 eggs
4 tablespoons water
   dash salt
⅓ cup whole wheat pastry flour
2 teaspoons *Baking Powder* (see index)
6 tablespoons carob powder
1 cup nuts, chopped

In a medium-sized mixing bowl, cream butter and sugar. Add vanilla, slightly beaten eggs, and water. Then add salt, flour, baking powder, carob and nuts. Mix well. Turn into well-greased 8-inch by 8-inch cake pan that is lined with waxed paper. Bake in preheated oven for 25 minutes. Cool and frost with *Carob Frosting* (see index).

Yield: 16 brownies

Note: As a rule I do not use even raw sugar, but for the rare times when I make brownies I prefer the texture attained with the sugar. You may follow the rule for converting recipes from sugar to honey if you wish.

Fig Bars
Preheat oven: 350°

> ¾ cup honey
> ¼ cup light molasses
> 3 eggs, beaten till foamy
> 1 cup whole wheat flour
> ½ cup wheat germ
> 1 teaspoon vanilla
> 1 teaspoon *Baking Powder* (see index)
> 1 cup figs, chopped
> ½ cup raisins
> sesame seeds for topping

> In a medium-sized mixing bowl, add honey and molasses to eggs. Add flour, wheat germ, vanilla and baking powder. Stir in figs and raisins. Pour into small, greased loaf pan. Sprinkle the top with sesame seeds. Bake in a preheated oven 30 to 35 minutes. Cool and cut into squares.

> Yield: 10-12 bars

Peanut Butter-Date Chews

> dates, pitted
> peanut butter
> almonds or pecans
> coconut, shredded (optional)

Flatten a date with a fork. Spread some peanut butter on top of it. Then place an almond or pecan in the center. Cover with another flattened and pitted date. Roll dates in coconut. Chill.

Honey-Date Bars
Preheat oven: 350°

¾ cup honey
¼ cup light molasses
2 eggs, beaten till foamy
¾ cup whole wheat flour
⅜ cup unbleached white flour
⅛ cup of wheat germ
1 teaspoon *Baking Powder* (see index)
  dash salt
1 cup nuts, chopped
1 teaspoon vanilla
1 cup dates, pitted and chopped

In a medium-sized mixing bowl, add honey and molasses to beaten eggs. Sift flours and wheat germ into a separate bowl. Mix baking powder, salt and nuts with flour. Add vanilla. Add flour mixture to honey mixture. Pour half the batter on the bottom of a greased, loaf pan. Cover with dates. Pour the other half of the batter on top. Bake in a preheated oven for 30 minutes. Cool and cut into squares.

Yield: 10 bars

Carob Chip Cookies
Preheat oven: 350°

½ cup butter, softened
1 cup honey
2 eggs, slightly-beaten
2¼ cups whole wheat flour
2 teaspoons *Baking Powder* (see index)
1 teaspoon salt
1 cup nuts, chopped
1 teaspoon vanilla
1 package carob chips

In a large mixing bowl, cream butter and honey. Add eggs. Add flour, baking powder, salt, nuts, vanilla and carob chips.
Mix well. Chill dough. Drop by teaspoonfuls on oiled cookie sheet. Bake in preheated oven, till lightly-browned (10 to 12 minutes).

Yield: 3 dozen

Date-Nut Balls (flourless)
Preheat oven: 300°

½ cup honey
1 egg
1 teaspoon vanilla
2 cups sunflower seed meal (made by grinding
1¼ cups sunflower seeds in blender)
1 teaspoon peanut butter (optional)
20 dates, pitted
bowl of sesame seeds for rolling

In a medium-sized mixing bowl, blend honey and egg. Add vanilla, sunflower seed meal and peanut butter. Stir well. Coat dates

174

with batter, which is fairly sticky, so be prepared for messy hands. Roll dates in sesame seeds. Place them on a cookie sheet and bake in preheated oven for about 10 minutes. Chill and serve.

Variations: 1. Use figs instead of dates. 2. Roll balls in coconut instead of sesame seeds. 3. Use 1 cup nutmeal and 1 cup sunflower meal in place of 2 cups sunflower seed meal. Yield: 20 balls

St. John's Patties
Preheat oven: 350°

1 cup honey
1 cup molasses
1 cup oil
1 cup carob powder
1 cup nuts, chopped
1 cup raisins, pitted dates, or figs, chopped
½ teaspoon ginger
1 teaspoon cinnamon
5 cups whole wheat flour
1 tablespoon Tiger's milk

In a large mixing bowl, mix all the ingredients together thoroughly. If batter is too sticky, add more flour. On a board, roll out the dough and cut it into patties. Flatten patties with a fork on a lightly-greased cookie sheet. Bake in a preheated oven for 12 minutes.

Variations: 1 cup coconut, ¼ teaspoon cloves, ¼ teaspoon mace or 1 teaspoon nutmeg and 1 cup any variety of nuts. Yield: 3½ dozen

175

Chinese Sesame Seed Cookies
Preheat oven: 375°

    1 cup butter
    4 cups whole wheat flour
    2½ teaspoons *Baking Powder* (see index)
    ¼ teaspoon salt
    ¾ cup honey
    2 eggs, slightly-beaten
    ¼ cup toasted sesame seeds
    1 teaspoon vanilla
    ¼ cup water
    ½ cup almonds, chopped

In a large mixing bowl, cut soft butter into flour, baking powder and salt. Add honey, eggs, sesame seeds, vanilla, water and almonds. Mix dough and chill 3 to 4 hours. On a board, roll out dough to ⅛-inch thick and cut it into cookies. Bake on a cookie sheet in preheated oven for about 10 minutes.

Yield: 4 dozen

Peanut Butter-Carob Candy (uncooked)

    4 cups peanut butter
    1½ cups honey
    1 cup nonfat dry milk
    2 tablespoons carob powder
    1 cup sunflower seeds
    1 cup raisins
    1 cup coconut shreds
    2 teaspoons vanilla

In a large mixing bowl, mix the ingredients

and press onto a 15½-inch by 10½-inch cookie sheet. Chill well and cut into bars or bite-sized pieces.　　Yield: 150, 1-inch squares

Oatmeal-Nut-Raisin Cookies
Preheat oven: 350°

1 cup honey
½ cup oil
2 eggs, slightly-beaten
½ ripe banana, mashed (optional)
1 teaspoon vanilla
1 teaspoon salt
2 teaspoons cinnamon
2 cups rolled oats
1 cup whole wheat flour (or ¾ wheat, ¼ soy)
2 teaspoons *Baking Powder* (see index)
½ cup pecans, chopped
½ cup almonds, chopped
1 cup raisins

In a large mixing bowl, mix honey and oil. Add eggs, then banana. Mix. Stir in vanilla, salt and cinnamon. Add rolled oats, flour, baking powder, nuts, and raisins. If mixture seems too dry, add a little milk to thin it out. If it is too sticky, add a little wheat germ to bind it. Drop batter by teaspoonfuls on a cookie sheet. Bake approximately 12 minutes in a preheated oven.

Variations: 1. Eliminate raisins and add 1 cup of chopped dates. 2. Reduce flour to ¾ of a cup and add 1 cup of coconut shreds. 3. Toast oats before using them.

　　　　　　　　　Yield: 4 dozen

Peanut Butter Cookies
Preheat oven: 300°

¼ cup oil
½ cup honey
¼ cup peanut butter
⅓ cup dates, chopped
½ teaspoon salt
⅓ teaspoon *Baking Powder* (see index)
1 cup whole wheat flour
½ cup nuts, chopped
20 pecans or almonds for centers (optional)

In a large mixing bowl, mix oil, honey, and peanut butter till smooth. Add the rest of the ingredients, except pecans. Drop by tablespoonfuls onto cookie sheet. Put a pecan (or almond) in the center of each. Bake about 10 to 15 minutes till lightly-browned in preheated oven. Do not over-bake.

Yield: 20 cookies

Rice Pudding I
Preheat oven: 325°

5½ cups brown rice, cooked (good way to use leftover rice)
3 eggs, beaten
¼ cup honey
¾ cup raisins
¼ cup dates, chopped
1 cup milk
½ cup coconut shreds
1 teaspoon cinnamon
¼ teaspoon salt
½ teaspoon nutmeg and cloves

In a large mixing bowl, mix all the ingredients. Bake in 2, oiled loaf pans in preheated oven for 45 minutes to 1 hour. Stir about every 15 minutes.

Yield: 10, 8-ounce servings

Rice Pudding II

- 4 cups milk
- ⅓ cup honey
  dash salt
- ½ cup brown rice, uncooked
- 1 cup raisins
- 5 eggs
- 2 teaspoons vanilla
- ¾ cup coconut shreds
- 1½ teaspoon cinnamon
- 1 teaspoon nutmeg
- 2 tablespoons butter

Mix in top of double boiler: milk, honey, and salt. Add rice and cook about 1½ hours. In a small saucepan, boil raisins in hot water. Remove raisins from heat and soak them for about 20 minutes. In a small mixing bowl, beat eggs and stir them into rice mixture. Drain water from raisins, and add them to rice, along with vanilla, and coconut. Pour into oiled baking dish. Top pudding with cinnamon and nutmeg, dot it with butter and bake it for 1 hour at 325°.

Yield: 8, 8-ounce servings

Bread Pudding

2 cups stale bread, chopped into small pieces
1 cup Mu tea
2 apples, cored and diced
½ cup nuts, chopped
½ cup raisins
1 teaspoon orange rind, grated
1 teaspoon cinnamon
1 tablespoon oil
1 egg, beaten
whole wheat flour if necessary to thicken

In large mixing bowl, soak the bread in the tea. Add the rest of the ingredients except egg and flour and let mixture stand 1 to 2 hours. Add beaten egg. If mixture is too runny, add flour or cooked cereal. Heat a large loaf pan in the oven. Remove the pan from oven, oil and flour it and pour in pudding batter. Bake in 325° oven until pudding pulls away from sides of the pan, about 45 minutes.

Yield: 6, 8-ounce servings

Raisin-Persimmon Pudding
Preheat oven: 325°

½ cup whole wheat flour
½ teaspoon salt
3 teaspoons *Baking Powder* (see index)
1 teaspoon ginger
2 teaspoons cinnamon
½ cup raisins
¼ cup figs, pitted and chopped
¼ cup dates, pitted and chopped
½ cup nuts, chopped
2 eggs, beaten
½ cup butter, melted
2 cups persimmon pulp
1 teaspoon vanilla

In a large mixing bowl, mix flour, salt, baking powder and spices. Add raisins, figs, dates, and nuts to flour mixture, stirring to separate pieces of fruit. In a separate bowl, combine eggs, butter, persimmon pulp and vanilla. Add liquid ingredients to dry ingredients. Blend well and pour batter into a greased casserole dish. Bake in preheated oven for 1½ hours.

Variation: Pitted prune puree may be substituted for persimmon pulp.

181

Apple Crisp

4 cups apples, sliced
1 cup raisins
½-¾ cup honey
2 tablespoons butter, melted
1 teaspoon lemon juice
1 tablespoon cinnamon
¾ cup oats
¼ cup whole wheat flour
dash salt

In a large mixing bowl, mix apples and raisins. Add honey, butter, lemon juice and cinnamon and let soak for about 30 minutes. In a small mixing bowl, mix oats, flour and salt. Lay apples, raisins and the honey mixture they soaked in, in a slightly-oiled, large, shallow baking dish. Spread oat mixture on top. Bake in a 325° oven for 40 to 45 minutes.

Variations: 1. Melt ¼ cup butter and mix with ½ cup honey. Pour on top of crisp before baking to give it a sweeter taste. 2. Add 1 cup chopped nuts. 3. Sprinkle wheat germ and sesame seeds on top of crisp. 4. Add coconut shreds to oat mixture.

Coffee Cake
Preheat oven: 350°

2 cups whole wheat flour
2 teaspoons *Baking Powder* (see index)
½ teaspoon salt
¾ cup honey
½ cup butter, softened
1 egg
1 cup yogurt
1 teaspoon vanilla
¼ cup raisins
¼ cup nuts, chopped (optional)

Secret Topping:
¼ cup milk
¼ cup butter
½ cup nuts, chopped
½ cup honey

In a large mixing bowl, sift flour, baking powder and salt together. Mix in ¾ cup of honey. Cut in ½ cup of butter with fork, 2 knives or pastry blender. In a small mixing bowl, beat egg and add it along with yogurt and vanilla, to flour. Add nuts and raisins. Pour into greased, 8-inch by 8-inch cake pan. In a small saucepan, bring milk, ¼ cup of butter and ½ cup of nuts to boil. Turn off heat and stir in ½ cup of honey. Pour topping over cake before baking in preheated oven for 30 minutes.

Variations: 1. Add ¾ teaspoon of grated lemon or orange rind. 2. Use almond extract instead of vanilla.

Coconut Coffee Cake
Preheat oven: 400°

> 1 cup honey
> ½ cup oil
> 3 eggs, beaten
> 1 teaspoon vanilla
> 1 cup milk
> 1½ cup whole wheat flour
> ½ cup wheat germ
> 1 tablespoon *Baking Powder* (see index)
> 1 teaspoon salt
> 1 teaspoon cinnamon
> ½ teaspoon nutmeg
> 1 cup coconut, grated
> ½ cup raisins (optional)

In a large mixing bowl, blend the honey, oil, eggs, vanilla, and milk. Set aside. In a medium-sized mixing bowl, combine the rest of the ingredients. Add dry ingredients, slowly, to the liquid mixture, just enough to make a stiff batter. Bake in a large, shallow pan in a preheated oven for 30 to 40 minutes. Ice with *Honey Coconut Frosting* (see index).

Apple Pudding Cake
Preheat oven: 350°

> 2 cups apples, peeled and sliced
> ¾ cup honey
> 1 egg, beaten
> ¾ cup nuts, chopped
> ½ cup raisins or dates, chopped and pitted

dash salt
4 teaspoons *Baking Powder* (see index)
1 teaspoon cinnamon
½ teaspoon allspice
1 teaspoon nutmeg
¼ cup butter, softened

In a large mixing bowl, combine all the ingredients. Pour batter into greased, square cake pan or a loaf pan. Bake in a preheated oven for 30 minutes.

Apple Sauce Cake
Preheat oven: 350°

1 cup honey
½ cup oil
1½ cups apple sauce, unsweetened
2 cups whole wheat flour (or 1½ cups wheat, ½ cup soy)
1 cup raisins
1 cup nuts, chopped
½ teaspoon cloves
1½ teaspoons cinnamon
½ teaspoon nutmeg
2 teaspoons *Baking Powder* (see index)

In a large mixing bowl, beat honey and oil till smooth. Add remaining ingredients, blending well. Turn batter into a large, oiled loaf pan and bake in preheated oven for 50 minutes.

Variation: Reduce raisins to ½ cup and add ½ cup chopped apple.

185

Apple Sauce Spice Cake
Preheat oven: 350°

½ cup oil
¾ cup honey
1⅓ cup apple sauce
¼ stick butter
1 teaspoon vanilla
2 cups whole wheat flour, sifted
1 teaspoon *Baking Powder* (see index)
2½ teaspoons cinnamon
½ teaspoon ground cloves
¼ teaspoon ginger
⅛ teaspoon allspice
¼ teaspoon nutmeg

In a large mixing bowl, blend the oil, honey and apple sauce. Cut butter into small squares and heat it in a medium-sized saucepan over low temperature until the butter is melted. Add the oil-honey-apple sauce mixture and stir until smooth. Add vanilla and stir. Remove from heat and return to mixing bowl. Add the sifted flour, baking powder and spices, blending well (batter will be a little sticky). Put batter in a greased and floured, 8-inch square pan and bake in a preheated oven for 30 to 40 minutes. Cool and top with *Applesauce Syrup* (see index).

Spice Cake
Preheat oven: 325°

⅔ cup oil
¾ cup honey
3 egg yolks, slightly beaten
¼ cup dry milk powder
¾ cup milk
2½ cups whole wheat flour
4 teaspoons *Baking Powder* (see index)
½ teaspoon salt
1 tablespoon cinnamon
½ teaspoon allspice
1 cup raisins
½ cup nuts, chopped
3 egg whites, stiffly beaten

In a large mixing bowl, blend oil and honey and add slightly-beaten egg yolks. In a small mixing bowl, stir milk powder into milk and add to honey and oil. Sift flour, baking powder, salt and spices together and add to mixture. Add raisins and nuts. Fold in stiffly beaten egg whites. Put batter in a large, oiled loaf pan and bake in preheated oven for 50 minutes.

Carob Cake
Preheat oven: 350°

1¼ cups honey
¼ cup oil
2 eggs, beaten
½ cup carob powder
½ cup boiling water
2½ cups whole wheat flour
3 teaspoons *Baking Powder* (see index)
1 teaspoon salt
1 teaspoon Pero (coffee substitute)
1 teaspoon vanilla
½ cup milk
1 cup nuts, chopped

In a large mixing bowl, blend honey and oil till smooth. Add eggs. In a small mixing bowl, dissolve carob powder in boiling water and add to honey. Sift flour, baking powder and salt and blend with honey mixture. Add Pero and vanilla. Stir in milk. Add nuts. Put batter in 2, 8-inch by 8-inch, oiled layer cake pans. Bake in preheated oven for 25 to 30 minutes. Ice with *Carob Frosting* (see index).

Carob Wedding Cake
Preheat oven: 350°

½ cup oil
1⅔ cups honey
2 egg yolks, beaten
½ cup carob powder
½ cup boiling water
2½ cups whole wheat flour
3 teaspoons *Baking Powder* (see index)
½ teaspoon salt
⅓ cup milk
⅓ cup cream
1 teaspoon Pero (coffee substitute)
1 teaspoon vanilla
1 cup nuts, chopped
2 egg whites, stiffly beaten

In a large mixing bowl, mix oil and honey. Add egg yolks. In a small mixing bowl, dissolve carob powder in boiling water and add to honey mixture. Sift flour, baking powder, salt and add them to mixture along with milk, cream, Pero, vanilla and nuts. Fold in stiffly beaten egg whites. Bake in a large, well-greased, oblong cake pan in preheated oven for 30 to 35 minutes. Ice with *Carob Frosting* or *Almond Icing* (see index).

Variations: 1. Add ½ cup shredded coconut to the batter. 2. Dissolve carob powder in cold water using a blender and add ½ medium-sized ripe banana.

Mock German Chocolate Cake
Preheat oven: 350°

    1¼ cups boiling water
    1 cup oats
    ½ cup butter
    2 tablespoons molasses
    1½ cups honey
    1 teaspoon vanilla
    2 eggs, slightly-beaten
    1½ cups whole wheat flour
    3 teaspoons *Baking Powder* (see index)
    ½ teaspoon salt
    ¼ teaspoon cinnamon
    ¼ teaspoon nutmeg

Pour water over oats in a large mixing bowl, and let stand for 20 minutes. Add butter, molasses, honey, vanilla and eggs. Blend till smooth. Sift together flour, baking powder and salt and add, with spices, to batter. Turn into large, shallow, greased cake pan, or 2 round cake pans for double layer cake. Bake in a preheated oven for 50 to 55 minutes. Ice single layer cake with *Coconut Icing* (see index). For double layer cake, use ½ of the recipe for *Almond Icing* (see index) for bottom layer, and use ½ of the recipe for *Coconut Icing* for the top.

Variations: 1. For a richer cake use granola instead of plain oats. 2. To serve in deluxe style: top with fresh strawberries before serving.

Refrigerator Fruit Cake

½ cup dates, chopped
½ cup figs, sliced
½ cup dried apricots or peaches, chopped
½ cup raisins or currants
½ cup nuts, chopped
½ cup sunflower seeds
3 tablespoons Tiger's milk
½ cup fresh coconut, grated
½ cup honey
¼ cup sesame seeds
½ cup apple juice
1 teaspoon cinnamon
½ teaspoon nutmeg
3 tablespoons apple juice
3 tablespoons wheat germ

In a large mixing bowl, combine all the ingredients except the 3 tablespoons of apple juice and the wheat germ. Press into large glass cake pan or loat pan lined with waxed paper. Brush the top with the 3 tablespoons of apple juice. Sprinkle the wheat germ on top. Let harden in refrigerator. This cake may be made several days in advance of serving.

Banana-Peanut Butter Cake
Preheat oven: 350°

¼ cup butter
¾ cup honey
1 egg
1 tablespoon peanut butter
3 ripe bananas, mashed
1 teaspoon vanilla
½ cup milk
2 cups whole wheat flour
1 tablespoon *Baking Powder* (see index)
¼ teaspoon salt
¾ cup nuts, chopped

In a large mixing bowl, cream butter and honey till smooth. Blend (in blender if possible) egg, peanut butter, bananas, vanilla and milk. Add this to honey and butter. Sift flour, baking powder and salt into a medium-sized mixing bowl and add, along with nuts, to first mixture. If batter seems thick, thin it out with a little milk. Turn into medium-sized, oiled cake pan and bake in preheated oven for 50 minutes. Cool and ice with *Carob Frosting*, *Peanut Butter Frosting*, or *Granola Topping* (see index).

Banana-Yogurt Cake
Preheat oven: 350°

¼ cup oil
1 cup honey
2 eggs, slightly-beaten
3 ripe bananas, mashed

3 tablespoons yogurt
1½ cup whole wheat flour
3 teaspoons *Baking Powder* (see index)
½ teaspoon salt
1 teaspoon nutmeg
1 teaspoon allspice
1 teaspoon vanilla

In a large mixing bowl, mix oil and honey till smooth. Blend in eggs. Add mashed bananas and yogurt and blend well. Sift in flour, baking powder and salt and add spices and vanilla. Turn into oiled, square cake pan. Bake in preheated oven for 45 minutes. Ice with *Carob Frosting*, *Peanut Butter Frosting*, or *Granola Topping* (see index).

Carrot Cake
Preheat oven: 300°

1 cup oil
1⅓ cups honey
4 eggs, beaten
1 teaspoon salt
3 teaspoons *Baking Powder* (see index)
2 cups whole wheat flour
3 cups carrots, grated or 2 cups carrots and
    1 cup pineapple, crushed and drained
1 cup nuts, chopped

In a large mixing bowl, blend all the ingredients thoroughly. Put batter into a large, well-greased bread pan. Bake in preheated oven for 40 to 50 minutes.

193

Gingerbread
Preheat oven: 350°

½ cup oil
1 cup honey
1 cup light molasses
1 cup cream
2 eggs
1 cup whole wheat flour
1⅛ cups unbleached white flour
⅜ cup wheat germ
1½ teaspoons *Baking Powder* (see index)
½ teaspoon salt
2 teaspoons ginger
½ teaspoon cloves
½ teaspoon cinnamon
1 cup nuts, chopped

In a large mixing bowl, blend oil, honey, molasses, and cream. Beat eggs and add. Sift flour, baking powder and salt together and add along with wheat germ to liquid ingredients. Add spices and nuts. Turn into large, oblong pan and bake in preheated oven for 50 minutes.

Variations: 1. Add 1 cup chopped apple. 2. Add 1 teaspoon grated lemon rind.

Almond Icing

1 cup almonds
1 tablespoon butter
⅓ cup honey
1 tablespoon milk
½ teaspoon vanilla

Chop almonds in blender till they are almond meal. Add butter, honey, milk and vanilla, and blend till thick. Add more milk or cream as needed to thin out to desired consistency.

Yield: ices 1, 10½-inch by 8½-inch cake

Carob Frosting

4 tablespoons honey
3 tablespoons butter, softened
⅔ cup nonfat dry milk powder
⅓ cup carob powder
4 tablespoons cream
½ teaspoon vanilla
½ cup nuts, chopped

In a medium-sized mixing bowl, cream honey and butter. Stir in milk powder and carob. Add cream and vanilla. Beat till smooth. Stir in nuts and spread over cake.

Yield: ices 2, 8-inch layer cakes
or 1 oblong cake

Quick Carob Frosting

6 tablespoons nonfat dry milk powder
4 teaspoons carob powder
4 teaspoons honey
1 teaspoon vanilla
  small amount of milk

In a small mixing bowl, combine all the ingredients and add enough milk, cream or water to thin out to frosting consistency.

Yield: ices 2, 8-inch layer cakes
or 1 oblong cake

Coconut Icing

½ cup honey
¼ cup butter, softened
3 tablespoons cream
½ cup nuts, chopped
¾ cup coconut, shredded

In a small mixing bowl, cream honey and butter. Beat until smooth. Add the remaining ingredients and mix in thoroughly. Spread on cake and slip under broiler for a few minutes to toast coconut and let other ingredients seep into cake.

Yield: ices 1 loaf cake or 1 square cake

Honey-Coconut Frosting

4 tablespoons butter, softened
4 tablespoons honey
2 tablespoons fresh coconut, grated
1 teaspoon vanilla

In a small mixing bowl, blend ingredients together well. Spread on top of coffee cake when it comes out of the oven. Slip under broiler for 3 minutes. Remove and cool cake before serving.

Yield: ices 1 coffee cake

Granola Topping

¾ cup oats
¾ cup coconut, shredded
½ cup nuts, chopped (optional)
¼ cup oil
1 teaspoon vanilla
small amount of honey

In a medium-sized mixing bowl, mix oats, coconut, nuts, oil and vanilla. Add enough honey to make topping sticky and sweet. Spread on top of cake before cake is baked. Makes a nice, chewy topping. May also be used as a topping after the cake is baked. (Slip the iced cake under broiler a few minutes.)

Yield: ices 1 large sheet cake

Peanut Butter Frosting

½ cup peanut butter
½ cup honey
½ ripe banana, mashed
1 tablespoon oil or butter
1 teaspoon vanilla

In a small mixing bowl, cream together all ingredients. Especially good on banana cakes.

Yield: ices 1 square cake

Buttermilk Syrup

⅔ cup honey
¼ teaspoon maple syrup
⅓ cup buttermilk
⅓ cup butter
½ teaspoon vanilla

In a small saucepan, combine all ingredients, except the vanilla. Boil over medium heat for 5 minutes. Remove from heat and add vanilla. Serve over *Carrot Cake* (see index).

Yield: approximately 1½ cups

Crumb Crust
Preheat oven: 350°

1½ cups whole wheat bread, cookie, graham cracker or granola crumbs
1 tablespoon sesame seeds
2 tablespoons sunflower seeds
¼ cup honey
6 tablespoons oil

In a medium-sized mixing bowl, combine crumbs, and seeds. In a small mixing bowl, mix honey and oil and pour over seeds and crumbs. Stir till all the crumbs are moist. Press into a well-greased, 9-inch pie pan with a spoon or your fingers. Bake in a preheated oven 12 to 15 minutes. Do not overbake. Good for custard, creme, pumpkin, and open-faced fruit pies.

Yield: 1, 9-inch crust

Delightful Apricot Turnovers

Filling:

1½ pounds dried, unsulphured apricots
honey to taste

In a large pot, cover dried apricots with cold water. Bring to a boil and simmer, uncovered, for 30 minutes. Sweeten with honey the last 5 minutes of cooking. Mash the apricots and honey into the cooking liquid.

Dough:

4 tablespoons butter
2 cups flour, whole wheat pastry, if possible
2 egg yolks
¼ teaspoon salt
6 tablespoons hot milk (do not boil)

In a large mixing bowl, cut butter into flour. In a small mixing bowl, combine egg yolks, salt, milk, and add to flour. On a board, knead well, using no extra flour. Roll dough about ⅛-inch thick and cut into 3½-inch diameter circles, using no flour on rolling pin. Fill each circle with 1 tablespoon filling. Fold in half and pinch edges together well. In a large skillet, saute turnovers in oil, at medium heat, till golden brown on each side. This should take about 5 to 10 minutes. Then bake 5 minutes at 425° on an ungreased cookie sheet.

Yield: 2 dozen

Apple Sauce Syrup

3 tablespoons butter
3 tablespoons berry jam or preserves
½ cup apple sauce
2 tablespoons honey
1 small apple, peeled, cored and grated

Place all ingredients in a saucepan. Boil 3 to 4 minutes. Serve hot on cake.

Whole Wheat Pie Crust

2 cups whole wheat flour (preferably pastry)
1½ cups unbleached white flour
½ cup wheat germ
2 cups safflower shortening or coconut oil, chilled
2 teaspoons salt
1 tablespoon honey
1 tablespoon apple cider vinegar
1 egg
½ cup water

In a large mixing bowl, mix flours and wheat germ well and cut shortening and salt into them with pastry blender, fork, or 2 knives. In a small mixing bowl, mix honey, vinegar, egg and water. Add to flour mixture and stir till moist. Shape into a ball and chill for 30 minutes. Roll out dough between waxed paper. (Freeze any leftover dough.)

Yield: 4, 9-inch or 5, 8-inch shells

3 Grain Pie Crust

1 cup unbleached white flour
¾ cup whole wheat flour
¼ cup soy flour
1 teaspoon salt
¼ cup sesame seeds
1 tablespoon wheat germ
¾ cup safflower shortening
4-5 tablespoons ice water

In a large mixing bowl, mix flours, salt, seeds and wheat germ. Cut in shortening with pastry blender, fork or 2 knives. Add water to make into dough. Chill before rolling out between 2 pieces of waxed paper.

Yield: 2, 9-inch pie crusts

Oatmeal Crust
Preheat oven: 375°

1 cup oats
½ cup whole wheat flour
¼ cup coconut, shredded
½ cup wheat germ or bran
¼ cup honey
4 tablespoons oil
1 teaspoon cinnamon
orange juice

In a medium-sized mixing bowl, mix first 7 ingredients and add enough orange juice to make dough. Press into well-greased pie pan and bake 12 to 15 minutes in a preheated oven. Fill crust with custard, creme, pumpkin, or use for open-faced fruit pies.

Yield: 1, 9-inch crust

Deep Dish Apple Pie
Preheat oven: 350°

10 medium-sized apples, thinly-sliced
½-¾ cup honey (depending on tartness of apples)
1 teaspoon cinnamon
½ teaspoon nutmeg
dash salt
squeeze of fresh lemon juice
2 tablespoons butter, melted
2 9-inch pie crusts

In a large mixing bowl, soak apples in the honey, cinnamon and nutmeg for an hour. Fill a pie shell with the apple mixture. Add salt and a squeeze of lemon juice. Dot with melted butter. Apples should come to about 1½ inch over the top of the pie pan. Put on top crust, prick well with a fork, or make a lattice top. Bake in preheated oven for about 50 minutes.

Hint: If apples are dry, add a little water, not much though because of the honey. If apples are extra juicy add 1 teaspoon flour.

Variations: 1. Add ½ cup of grated carrot. 2. Add ½ to 1 cup of raisins.

Banana Custard Pie

⅓ cup honey
1 tablespoon whole wheat or soy flour
  dash salt
3 egg yolks, slightly-beaten
2 cups scalded milk*
1 teaspoon vanilla
  baked pie shell
1 large banana, sliced
  coconut and/or toasted wheat germ to garnish

Mix honey, flour and salt in the top of a double boiler. Add egg yolks and milk. Add vanilla and cook about 15 minutes over medium heat till mixture thickens. Stir occasionally. Cover bottom of 9-inch baked pie shell with banana slices. Add custard and garnish with coconut and/or toasted wheat germ.

For Coconut Custard Pie: Add 1 cup of toasted coconut shreds after removing custard from heat.

*Scalded milk—bubbling around the edges, under the boiling point.

Strawberry-Banana Pie

1-1½ cups fresh strawberries
⅓ cup honey
3 medium-sized bananas, ripe but firm
1 baked, 9-inch *Crumb Crust* or *Oatmeal Crust*
(see index)
1 egg white
½ cup honey
½ teaspoon vanilla

Remove stems and slice strawberries. In a small mixing bowl, soak them in ⅓ cup honey. Slice the bananas. Line a crumb crust with the bananas and then with the strawberries and the honey they were soaked in. In a medium-sized mixing bowl, beat an egg white till stiff, and slowly add ½ cup honey. Beat thoroughly about 10 to 12 minutes and add vanilla. Pour over berries and chill.

Yeasted Berry Pie

Dough:

Use ½ recipe for *Honey Wheat Bread* (see index). Divide this in half and roll ½ very thin with rolling pin. Line a lightly-greased pie pan with it. Pour 1 tablespoon of butter in center of dough and spread, coating with a spoon.

Filling:

3-4 cups fresh berries
¾ cup honey
1 teaspoon lemon juice

2 tablespoons arrowroot starch (used for thick-
    ening; use cornstarch in a pinch)

In a large mixing bowl, mix filling ingredients
together. Roll out other half of the dough
very thin for top crust or slice it into thin
strips for a lattice crust. Pour filling into pie
shell and top with crust. Pinch edges together
to seal well. Slit with a knife around the center if top crust is used. Bake at 450° for 10
minutes. Reduce heat to 350° and bake 30
minutes longer.

Pecan Pie
Preheat oven: 350°

1 tablespoon whole wheat flour
1 teaspoon salt
2 eggs, slightly-beaten
1 cup light molasses or maple syrup
½ cup honey
⅓ cup butter, melted
1 cup pecans, chopped
  few drops of vinegar (white or cider)
1 teaspoon vanilla
1 9-inch unbaked pie shell

In a medium-sized mixing bowl, add flour
and salt to beaten eggs. Mix well. Add
molasses, honey, and butter. Then add
pecans, vinegar and vanilla. Put into pie shell
and bake in a preheated oven for 45 minutes.

Carob Creme Pie

¾ cup honey
½ cup whole wheat flour
  dash salt
3 cups milk
4 tablespoons carob powder
2 egg yolks, beaten
1 teaspoon vanilla
1 9-inch baked pie shell (see index)

Mix honey, flour and salt in top of double boiler. In a small saucepan, scald milk*, adding carob to milk when scalding. Add scalded milk to flour and honey mixture. Cook about 15 minutes till mixture starts to thicken. Add egg yolks, and vanilla. Mix and cook a few more minutes. Pour into a baked pie shell. Chill till firm.

For *Banana Carob Creme Pie:* Cover baked pie shell bottom with sliced bananas.

*Scalded milk—bubbling around the edges, under the boiling point.

Peach Pie
Preheat oven: 350°

½-¾ cup honey (depending on sweetness of peaches)
4 tablespoons whole wheat flour
4 cups peaches, sliced (not too juicy)
  dash salt
  dash nutmeg
  dash ginger
2 9-inch, unbaked pie shells or *Crumb Crust*

In a large mixing bowl, combine honey and flour. Add sliced peaches, salt and spices. Roll out 2, 9-inch crusts, 1 for bottom, 1 for top (pricked well) or make a crumb crust bottom, fill and bake open-faced in a pre-heated oven for about 40 minutes.

Rhubarb Pie (tart)
Preheat oven: 350°

3 cups rhubarb, chopped
1-1½ cups honey (add more if desired)
½ teaspoon ginger
¼ teaspoon mace
1 teaspoon lemon juice
1 tablespoon whole wheat flour
2 9-inch, unbaked pie shells

In a medium-sized mixing bowl, mix all ingredients and fill pie shell. Add a top crust, pricked well, or a lattice top. Bake in preheated oven 40 to 50 minutes.

Sautéed Bananas

3 bananas, sliced or mashed
3 tablespoons butter
3 tablespoons honey
1 tablespoon peanut butter (optional)

Slice bananas lengthwise and cook in a skillet, in butter over low temperature until browned. Add honey and peanut butter to coat bananas.

Variation: Bake bananas 5 to 10 minutes at 250° after sautéing them.

Fruit Banana Splits

In a banana split dish, put a few scoops of *Sweet Summer Fiesta Salad* (see index). Cut a banana in half, lengthwise and lay half on each side of dish. Top with yogurt and sprinkle with chopped nuts.

Stuffed Baked Apples

For each serving:
1 apple
1 teaspoon raisins
1 teaspoon dates or figs, chopped
1 teaspoon nuts, chopped
1 teaspoon butter, melted (optional)
1 tablespoon honey
  dash cinnamon
2 tablespoons water

Wash and core apples leaving ¼ inch on the bottom to hold filling inside. In a mixing bowl, make a filling by combining raisins, dates and nuts. Fill core with mixture and pour the butter and honey into each core. Sprinkle with cinnamon. Wrap each apple in foil with the water, place in a shallow baking dish and bake in a 400° oven about 30 minutes (till tender).

Variation: Wash and core apples, peel skin half way down and fill with filling as above. Lay apples in a baking dish with ⅓ inch of water on the bottom. Cover the dish with foil and bake.

Index

Index

How to do <u>almost</u> everything

W hat are the latest time and money-saving shortcuts for painting, papering, and varnishing floors, walls, ceilings, furniture? (See pages 102-111 of HOW TO DO *Almost* EVERYTHING.) What are the mini-recipes and the new ways to make food—from appetizers through desserts—exciting and delicious? (See pages 165-283.) How-to-do-it ideas like these have made Bert Bacharach, father of the celebrated composer (Burt), one of the most popular columnists in America.

This remarkable new book, HOW TO DO *Almost* EVERYTHING, is a fact-filled collection of Bert Bacharach's practical aids, containing thousands of tips and hints— for keeping house, gardening, cooking, driving, working, traveling, caring for children. It will answer hundreds of your questions, briefly and lucidly.

How to do <u>almost</u> everything

is chock-full of useful information—information on almost everything you can think of, arranged by subject in short, easy-to-read tidbits, with an alphabetical index to help you find your way around —and written with the famed Bacharach touch.

SEND FOR YOUR FREE EXAMINATION COPY TODAY

We invite you to mail the coupon below. A copy of HOW TO DO *Almost* EVERYTHING will be sent to you at once. If at the end of ten days you do not feel that this book is one you will treasure, you may return it and owe nothing. Otherwise, we will bill you $7.95, plus postage and handling. At all bookstores, or write to Simon and Schuster, Dept. S-52, 630 Fifth Ave., New York, N.Y. 10020.

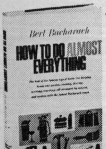

SIMON AND SCHUSTER, Dept. S-52
630 Fifth Ave., New York, N.Y. 10020

Please send me a copy of HOW TO DO *ALMOST* EVERYTHING. If after examining it for 10 days, I am not completely delighted, I may return the book and owe nothing. Otherwise, you will bill me for $7.95 plus mailing costs.

Name...

Address...

City..................State........Zip.......

☐ *SAVE!* Enclose $7.95 now and we pay postage. Same 10-day privilege with full refund guaranteed. (N. Y. residents please add applicable sales tax.)

P 66/2

VOLUME TWO

(Over 1,000,000 copies of Volume one sold)

THE WAY THINGS WORK

From aerosols to video tape recording. 1,057 two-color drawings. Clear, concise explanations.

How do aerosols work? (See page 20 of THE WAY THINGS WORK, VOLUME TWO.) How is foam plastic made? (See page 52.) How can the performance of your automobile's engine be improved? (See page 260.) How does the color get into TV? (See page 288.) What is inertial navigation? (See page 374.) How do safety bindings on skis protect you? (See page 444.) What are the different methods of video tape recording? (See page 560.)

This remarkable book will answer hundreds of your questions (and the "hows" and "whys" your children ask) about theories and their practical application in machines that, seen or unseen, are part of our everyday lives.

Now you can know *The Way Things Work*

Here are concise, carefully detailed descriptions of the principles and the working parts of musical instruments, industrial metallurgy, ballistics, wing geometry, ship stabilizing, automotive engineering, computers, generators—in short, of hundreds of things small and large, simple and complex, that make you wonder, "How does it work?"

And those who *didn't* read Volume One will surely want to take advantage of our offer to obtain *both* of these invaluable reference books that explain the marvels of technology that daily fill our world.

The books that satisfy the curiosity most of us feel when we push a button, or throw a switch, or turn a knob on any one of the hundreds of appliances and machines that surround us with their mysteries.

Send for your free examination copy today

We invite you to mail the coupon. A copy of Volume Two of THE WAY THINGS WORK will be sent to you at once. If at the end of ten days you do not feel that this book is one you will treasure, you may return it and owe nothing. Otherwise, we will bill you for $11.95 plus mailing costs. At all bookstores, or write to Simon and Schuster, Dept. S-54, 630 Fifth Avenue, New York, N.Y. 10020.

SIMON AND SCHUSTER, Dept. S-54
630 Fifth Avenue, New York, N.Y. 10020

☐ Send me a copy of *Volume Two* of THE WAY THINGS WORK. If after examining it for 10 days I am not completely delighted, I may return the book and owe nothing. Otherwise, you will bill me for $11.95 plus mailing costs.

☐ Send me for 10 days' free examination, a copy of *Volume One*, at $11.95 plus mailing costs. Same return privilege.

Name..

Address...

City..State............................Zip...............

☐ SAVE. Enclose payment now and publisher pays mailing costs. Same 10-day return privilege with full refund guaranteed. (New York residents please add applicable sales tax.)

P 67/2